MW01098331

IMAGES
of America

MEXICAN AMERICAN
BOXING IN LOS ANGELES

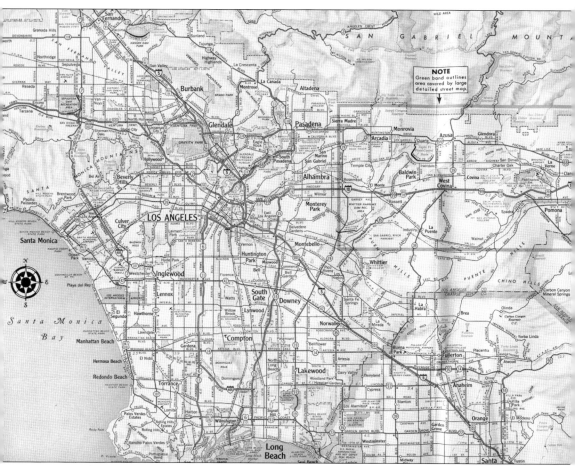

This 1962 map covers the Greater Los Angeles area, where the majority of boxers in this book trained, fought, and lived. Downtown Los Angeles was the home of the Olympic Auditorium and Main St. Gym, making Southern California fertile ground for some of the best fighters that ever stepped into the ring.

ON THE COVER: This image shows young Mexican American boxer Herman "Kid" Montes in only his eighth fight at the Olympic Auditorium. It also captures the underlying emotions and drama that can occur inside the ring. Sponsor Bob Castillo (far left) took Montes as far as possible and was being replaced by new manager Bennie Georgino (behind Montes), father/trainer John Montes Sr. (second from left) worked his son's corner, and referee John Thomas (second from right) raises Montes's arm, signifying victory. (Author's collection.)

IMAGES
of America

MEXICAN AMERICAN
BOXING IN LOS ANGELES

Gene Aguilera

ARCADIA
PUBLISHING

Published by Arcadia Publishing
Charleston, South Carolina

Printed in the United States of America

Library of Congress Control Number: 201394360

For all general information, please contact Arcadia Publishing:
Telephone 843-853-2070
Fax 843-853-0044
E-mail sales@arcadiapublishing.com
For customer service and orders:
Toll-Free 1-888-313-2665

Visit us on the Internet at www.arcadiapublishing.com

*This book is dedicated with forever love to my daughters
Emily Aguilera and Melanie Aguilera, also to my "Mama"
Carmen Aguilera and Aunt Maggie Cano.*

CONTENTS

ACKNOWLEDGMENTS

The author would like to thank Maria "Chuyita" Aguilera, Emily Aguilera, Melanie Aguilera, and Monica Felix; Jeff Ruetsche, Jared Nelson, Elizabeth Bray, and Tim Sumerel of Arcadia Publishing; Ruben "El Puas" Olivares, Elba Aguilar Olivares, "Mr. B." Jim Berklas, Lynn Berklas, Bob Recendez, Carlos Baeza, George Rodriguez, Rudy Tellez, Bert Sugar, Don Fraser, Dan Hanley, Richard Orozco, Frank "kiki" Baltazar Sr., and Jose J. Ramirez; his family—Lorenzo Aguilera Jr., Ernest Aguilera, Julie Gillis, Jack Robledo, Debbie (Gillis) Rose, Eric Cazarez, Janelle Cazarez, Christien Cazarez, Lauri (Aguilera) Rey, Robert Aguilera, and Chuck Aguilera; boxer friends Mando Ramos, Armando Muniz, Carlos Palomino, Danny "Little Red" Lopez, Joey Olivo, Oscar "The Boxer" Muniz, Frankie Duarte, Johnny "Wito" Montes, Herman "Kid" Montes, Arturo Frias, Paul Gonzales, "Zeffie" Gonzalez, Danny Valdez, Ruben Castillo, Bobby Chacon, Alberto "Superfly" Sandoval, Rodolfo "El Gato" Gonzalez, Oscar De La Hoya, Chiquita Gonzalez, Ricardo "Finito" Lopez, Pipino Cuevas, Carlos Zarate, Alfonso Zamora, Orlando Canizales, Gaspar "El Indio" Ortega, "Mighty" Mike Anchondo, Rudy "Chicano" Hernandez, Rick Farris, Ersi Arvizu, and Leonard Siqueiros; Ed Brophy and Jeff Brophy of the International Boxing Hall of Fame; Fernando Ballin, Greg Schultz, Mike Archuleta, Hank Kaplan, Jack Hirsch, Joey Fiato, Melanie Fiato, Michael "Spike" Wiles, Jo Jo Torres, Tony Rivera, Dan Goossen, Jose Vazquez De La Torre, Johnny "Flash" Ortiz, Don Chargin, Lorraine Chargin, Jimmy Lennon Jr., John Beyrooty, Carol Steindler, Javier Ruiz, Fernando Garcia, Mario Bustamante, James Salas, Jorge Ruiz, Jose Ruiz, Chris Gaffney, Dave Alvin, Little Willie G., Larry Rendon, Ry Cooder, Jackson Browne, Cesar Rosas, Manuel Gonzales, "Kid" Ramos, Richard "Scar" Lopez, Mario Lobato, Allen Larman, Big Sandy, Rudy Regalado, Little Joe Hernandez, Raul Jaimes, Frank Acosta, Joe "5.0" Garcia, Eddie "The Tailor" Garcia, Tudy Galvan, DeAnn Valdez, Ernesto Peralta, Craig Newnes, Richard Diaz, A.J. Lopez, Oscar Valdez, Rudy Montano, Adolfo Perez, Juan Silva, Alan Swyer, Lou Manfra, Craig Hamilton, Joey Santomarco, Peter Tomlinson, Keith Stechman, John Gay, Fred Romano, Don Crutchfield, referee Michael Ortega, Ignacio De La Vega, Domenic Priore, Roberto Haro, Oscar Zeta Acosta, Harvey Kubernik, Joe Adame, Froylan Corona Montiel, Keith Kizer, John Flynn, Community Commerce Bank, Telacu, John Sheppard at Boxrec.com, *Sports Illustrated*, the *Ring*, the *Los Angeles Herald Examiner*, and the *Los Angeles Times*.

INTRODUCTION

A couple of years ago while cleaning out my garage, I found a scrapbook my family had bought for me at Disneyland back in 1961. While looking through this personal gem, I saw all the things that were important to me as a young boy. Throughout my early years, I had cut and glued pictures of all my favorite Los Angeles sports teams (Dodgers, Angels, Rams, and Lakers), the British Invasion musical groups (Beatles, Dave Clark Five, Searchers, Gerry and the Pacemakers), and monster hot rod builder Ed "Big Daddy" Roth.

But tucked away on one of the pages were two pictures with captions that read "Champion Cassius Clay" and "Sonny Liston." There it was—I needed no more proof. When Clay (Ali) first beat Liston for the world heavyweight title in 1964, I was 10 years old and boxing was flowing through my veins.

My intention with this book is to capture the colorful, flamboyant, and wonderful world of *Mexican American Boxing in Los Angeles*. From the minute they step into the ring, Mexican American fighters have electrified fans with their explosiveness and courage. Their big hearts provide for sensational ring wars—never a dull moment here, folks. Don't go buy a beer, because by the time you get back, the fight might be over! Local Los Angeles Mexican American boxers, such as Bobby Chacon and Frankie Duarte, knew that to give a punch, they had to take a punch.

You read about boxing in the *Los Angeles Herald Examiner*. You saw the gorgeous "floating head" boxing posters on the telephone poles. You went to the Olympic Auditorium to root for your favorite fighter. Chicano boxers rubbing elbows with Hollywood celebrities—it was a sociological culture all of its own. Fans idolized and shrewd promoters drooled over these Mexican American boxers that did battle every second of every round. And if the fight ended in a knockout? Well, that's even better. This type of aggressive boxing obviously made it easier for Los Angeles promoters, like Aileen Eaton and Don Fraser, to pack 'em in, giving the fans their money's worth.

To a boxing fan, it is the greatest sport in the world. A boxer is an isolated gladiator in the ring, no teammates to help out, only your opponent stands in front of you. Promoter George Parnassus said, "In boxing it is one man by himself, against one man, all alone. That is what it comes down to, does it not, to know which man is best?" An understated irony is that one minute you are at war and the next minute you are hugging like best of friends, like turning off a light switch.

It's sportsmanship at its highest degree. Boxing is a sport of technique, skill, and wit. It can pit scientific boxing vs. brute strength in sports' purest form of competition. To quote musician Ry Cooder from his CD *Chavez Ravine*, "The Olympic Auditorium, downtown, was the top-of-the-line venue for East L.A. fighters in those days. But your life can change at the end of one punch." Like a good novella with highs and lows, twists and turns, you can't shake loose from the sport. Prefight hype can swallow you up, sometimes making the buildup better than the bout itself. But, ultimately, the relationship between boxers and fans is closer than any other sport.

From saving newspaper clippings of my favorite Mexican American boxers to hanging out at the Main St. Gym, from listening to bar talk of fans arguing who's the best to watching Saturday night fights on Channel 34 from Mexico, and from going to the Olympic Auditorium and the Fabulous Forum to the bright lights of Las Vegas, I have, unknowingly, been preparing all my life to write this book. It is a blessing to make a yearly pilgrimage to the holy land of boxing, the International Boxing Hall of Fame in Canastota, New York, accompanying the greatest bantamweight of all time, Ruben Olivares.

One cannot ignore the immense contributions of boxers that came from Mexico, and they must be integrated within the fiber of this book. Many Mexican-born fighters crossed over at an early age, made the Los Angeles area their home, and became local stars to the Mexican

American public. The popularity and success of boxers from Mexico goes hand in hand with *Mexican American Boxing in Los Angeles*; one cannot exist without the other.

With the burgeoning Mexican population in the Los Angeles area, it's no surprise that warriors from south of the border migrated north for their fame and fortune. They engaged in some of the most exciting and entertaining boxing matches ever to take place in Los Angeles while instilling pride in the hearts of the growing Southland Latino community. Perhaps the greatest fight I ever saw live was "The Battle of the Zs," the Carlos Zarate–Alfonso Zamora bombs-away war at the Forum in 1977.

The historical legacy of Los Angeles boxing will forever be tied in with the epic showdowns held between tough, game Mexican American boxers against beloved Mexican ring idols—together bringing in huge gate-drawing power. Slugfests such as Herman Montes (US) vs. Pipino Cuevas (MEX) and Bobby Chacon (US) vs. Ruben Olivares (MEX) come to mind, providing a heartfelt international flavor that was enticing to fans from both sides of the border.

Mexican American boxing fans are loyal to the end. Their love and embrace of a hometown hero never fades away. A new world champion instinctively carried himself with a noble aura that parlayed into a celebrity status in town. There were real neighborhood rivalries that existed and it was barrio vs. barrio to protect your turf. From Chavez Ravine, you had Carlos Chavez and Vince Delgado. The poster read "Harbor vs. Maravilla" when Chicano icon Mando Ramos fought Ruben Navarro. "Schoolboy" Bobby Chacon represented the San Fernando Valley, and from the "Big Hazard" gang you had Eddie "The Animal" Lopez and Joey Olivo. The nicknames were just as fabulous as the fighters themselves: "Little Red" Lopez, "King" Carlos, Armando "The Man," and "Superfly" Sandoval, just to name a few.

There was a romantic notion surrounding *the golden age* of boxing in Los Angeles during the 1940s and 1950s. Los Angeles was a hotbed of boxing back then. Local matchmaker Hap Navarro fondly remembered, "Los Angeles, one of the world's greatest boxing cities, has probably developed more sensational box-office attractions than any other city," and boxing beat writer John Beyrooty recalled the days "when Los Angeles was truly a fight town." A central figure to the story is "Golden Boy" Art Aragon. Like a winding thread, Aragon bobs and weaves throughout the book. Aragon's heart will always occupy a huge section of the Olympic Auditorium. He may never have made it to a world title, but he was the Olympic box office champion of the 1950s.

This is not meant to be the definitive picture book on Mexican American boxing in Los Angeles. It is physically impossible to mention every boxer of Mexican descent who laced up gloves in the Greater Los Angeles area. But what we have attempted to do, through the world of pictures, is capture the spirit and keep the legacy alive of the many great Mexican American fighters who did battle in the ring for their families, friends, and neighborhoods. And as we know, every picture tells a story.

Now shake hands and come out fighting.

One

THE 1900s–1930s
THERE WAS MURDER IN HIS EYES

He could hit as hard as Jim Jeffries although he was only a lightweight. He landed one of his famous punches that almost tore the top of my head off. I have never been hit as hard before or since. I turned a complete somersault and fell flat on my back. I looked up and saw Herrera standing over me with murder in his eyes. That happened in the fifth round. Around the 17th round my head cleared . . . but I could not recall anything that happened in those 12 rounds. I really think Herrera was the greatest man I met.

—Battling Nelson, world lightweight champion, describing his
September 5, 1904, bout with Aurelio Herrera.

Before he became a boxer, Aurelio Herrera was one of the best card dealers in a wild little town way out west known as Bakersfield, California. However, Herrera's reputation of having heavy fists quickly became the talk of the gambling house. Herrera's knockout exploits soon cut a path in the Northwest and, eventually, across the United States while carrying the shield for all hard-drinking boxers. Herrera displayed a cold confidence and disinterested air that bothered his opponents. He should be remembered as Southern California's first boxing Latino superstar.

Featherweight "Baby" Arizmendi's signature victory over all-time boxing great Henry Armstrong on November 4, 1934, is described in a newspaper account: "Arizmendi's superior boxing and effective body punching enabled him to win almost every round . . . Fighting with a broken left wrist from the second round, Arizmendi gave one of the most courageous exhibitions in Mexican ring history."

There were tales of oddities from the Wild West era, such as police stoppages of bouts when a boxer became hopelessly hurt, 20-round fights, imposter opponents, and boxing matches being declared "no contest" because of lack of action or stalling from the combatants. Then there were the "newspaper decisions," meaning if there was no knockout or clear-cut winner by the fight's conclusion, the bout was officially declared a "no decision." However, newspaper reporters seated at ringside would decide their own "winner" and print their results the following day.

Aurelio Herrera was one of the hardest-hitting lightweight boxers ever and a trailblazer for Mexican American fighters of his era. He is seen below at right in his 1904 bout with Battling Nelson. Fighting out of Bakersfield, Herrera inflicted true terror into the hearts of his opponents. Herrera began his career in 1895, frequently fought at Los Angeles boxing venues, and retired in 1909 with a record of 66 wins (59 knockouts), 12 losses, and 14 draws. It was said that he hit as hard as a safe, "but he liked wine, women, and long-black cigars better than ring fame," according to an article in *Boxing and Wrestling* magazine. Herrera was described by fellow boxers as the greatest one-punch knockout artist ever seen and won the featherweight championship of the Northwest on February 5, 1903, with a 10th-round TKO over Kid Oglesby at the Grand Theatre in Butte, Montana. On May 29, 1901, Herrera was knocked out in the fifth round in his only attempt at the world title by featherweight champion "Terrible" Terry McGovern at Mechanic's Pavilion in San Francisco. After the fight, Herrera mysteriously claimed he was doped by one of his seconds.

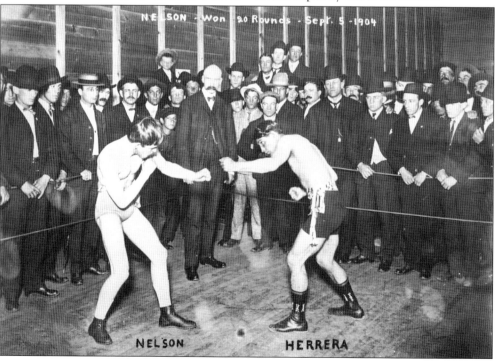

NELSON — Won 20 Rounds - Sept. 5 -1904

NELSON   HERRERA

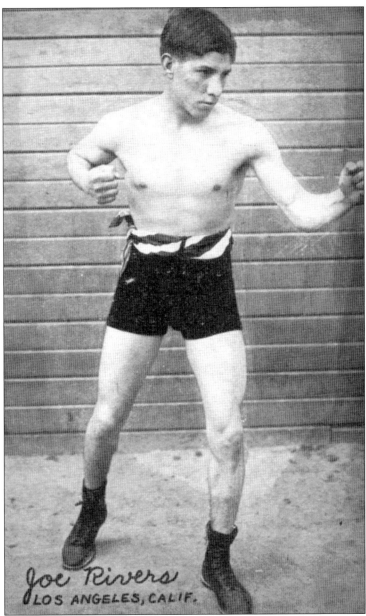

Joe Rivers
LOS ANGELES, CALIF.

"Mexican" Joe Rivers, born Jose Ybarra in Los Angeles, was a lightning-quick lightweight boxer who fought from 1908 to 1924, ending with a record of 38 wins (20 knockouts), 24 losses, and 13 draws. A big drawing card at the Vernon Arena, Rivers claimed the world featherweight title with a 13th-round TKO over Joe Coster on July 4, 1911. Rivers was a flashy character who drove a new Simplex touring car and sported expensive rings. On July 4, 1912, Rivers fought champion Ad Wolgast of Michigan for the world's lightweight title in front of a full house at the Vernon Arena. In one of the most controversial decisions in boxing history, both fighters landed a rare simultaneous double knockdown in the 13th round with Wolgast proceeding to fall on top of Rivers. Referee Jack Welch, who was handpicked by Wolgast, began an abbreviated count on Rivers while helping Wolgast up and declared him the winner by knockout. After the fight, bedlam ensued with referee Welch running for his life.

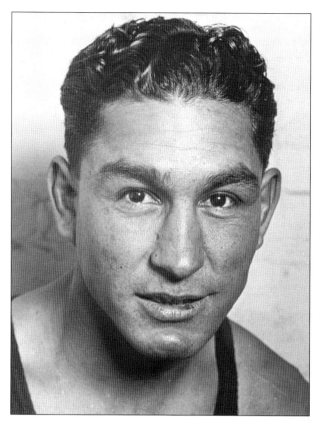

Bert Colima possessed an elegant fighting style that helped him capture the Pacific Coast middleweight championship in 1924 and the Mexican national welterweight title in 1928. In a career that spanned from 1919 to 1933, "The Whittier Bearcat," born Epifanio Romero in the Los Nietos neighborhood of West Whittier, was the most popular Mexican American boxing attraction at Jack Doyle's Vernon Arena, located at Thirty-eighth and Santa Fe Avenue. He changed his last name to Colima (in honor of his grandmother's hometown in Mexico) at the convincing of his manager. Colima was a top-ranked welterweight contender who fought all the way to the light heavyweight division, ending with a record of 144 wins (55 knockouts), 37 losses, and 22 draws. Below, Colima (right) poses in the ring with an unidentified heavyweight boxer in 1928.

Bert Colima (right) squares off against ace welterweight champion Mickey Walker "The Toy Bulldog" (left) for their nontitle tiff at the Vernon Arena on February 24, 1925. When Walker (with heavyweight champion Jack Dempsey, far left, holding coat) dropped "The Whittier Flash" in the seventh round, Dutch Meyers (Colima's manager) applied smelling salts to his downed fighter during referee Harry Lee's count. Colima was promptly disqualified and an angry protest ensued.

Los Angeles–born Richie Lemos was a southpaw featherweight boxer who won the NBA world featherweight title with a fifth-round knockout over defending champion Petey Scalzo of New York at the Olympic Auditorium on July 1, 1941. After the fight, Lemos was greeted with a hug and kiss in the ring by popular Mexican film actress Lupe Velez. Lemos fought from 1937 to 1943, ending with a record of 55 victories (26 knockouts), 23 losses, and 3 draws.

World featherweight champion Alberto "Baby" Arizmendi (center) doles out advice to young amateur boxers Carlos Chavez (left) and his older brother Alfredo Chavez (right) in 1934. Both Chavez brothers, who later turned professional, pose with Arizmendi at the original Main St. Gym, which was located at 321 South Main Street in Los Angeles, before it burned down in 1951. Arizmendi, possibly at age 14 the youngest boxer to turn professional, went on to become Mexico's first boxing star. Newspapers described Arizmendi as "displaying all the speed and agility of his Aztec ancestry" when "the brown idol of Old Mexico and Little Mexico alike" decisively took a 10-round decision defeating Newsboy Brown of Los Angeles for the world featherweight title (as recognized by the California Athletic Commission) at the Olympic Auditorium on October 18, 1932. Born in Torreón, Coahuila, Mexico, Los Angeles fan–favorite Arizmendi also captured the NYSAC world featherweight title in 1932 and the California-Mexico world featherweight title in 1935. Arizmendi fought from 1927 to 1942 and closed out his career with 84 wins (19 knockouts), 26 losses, and 14 draws.

Two

THE 1940s
BOMBS AWAY ON THE WEST COAST

Enrique Bolanos was far and away the most popular fighter Los Angeles ever knew. No one has ever come close. He had a 'look' like no other. You would have had to see it to know what I mean. It was the 'look' his fans saw and loved. There will never be another like him.

—Johnny Ortiz, boxing journalist, as told to David A. Avila of the Sweet Science website

This was the beginning of *the golden age* of Los Angeles boxing. The 1940s were the prime time of bantamweight champion Manuel Ortiz, who impressively dominated his division. They were also the glory days of beloved lightweight contender Enrique Bolanos. The West Coast swing era officially kicked in. With Pachuco swagger, zoot suits and khakis pressed tight, they spent their money as fast as they made it.

From Corona, California, came Manuel Ortiz, who was the two-time bantamweight titleholder for eight years (1942–1950), except for a brief two-month span in 1947. At the time, only heavyweight champion Joe Louis had more title defenses than Ortiz, who had a total of 21 during his reign. Ortiz's spectacular run as monarch of the bantam division included jumping up in weight class to fight such featherweights as Willie Pep and Enrique Bolanos. Ortiz said Los Angeles featherweight Carlos Chavez was his toughest opponent in his career. Local boxing writers raved, "Ortiz and Chavez fought like wildcats and the referee never had to break them."

Bolanos was a huge Mexican American favorite here after World War II. Matchmaker Hap Navarro wrote of the charismatic Bolanos, "There were few moments in my active boxing life that compare with the thrill of watching this brilliant boxer, one of the best to grace a California ring, unfurl his heart and soul before an adoring audience." Bolanos recalled to the *Los Angeles Times*, "If I were born again, I would still be a boxer . . . I trained hard for the fights, but I had a lot of fun, too. I was young and crazy. I went to dives, thinking George wouldn't be able to find me, but he always did." Manager George Parnassus saw Bolanos as a son, "but look at my white hair, he put 90 percent of them there."

Manuel Ortiz, two-time world bantamweight champion, battled in the ring from 1938 to 1955 and, while in his prime, held the indoor gate records for Los Angeles and Mexico City. Considered one of the best boxers of the 1940s, Ortiz first won the bantamweight title on August 7, 1942, when he outpointed defending champion Lou Salica of Brooklyn, New York, at Hollywood Legion Stadium in a 12-round unanimous decision. Ortiz had an incredible record of 21 wins with only 2 losses in title fights and will go down as one of the most active world champions in the history of boxing. Bantamweight kingpin Ortiz was a fighting machine who ended with a record of 101 victories (54 knockouts), 28 losses, and 3 draws. Below, Ortiz relaxes while reading the newspaper during World War II.

Talented lightweight contender Enrique Bolanos was the top draw for fans of the Los Angeles boxing scene from 1941 to 1952. Bolanos, of Durango, Mexico, fought regularly at the Olympic Auditorium and Hollywood Legion Stadium, chalking up 79 wins (44 knockouts), 22 losses, and 5 draws during his illustrious career. Even though Bolanos won the California state lightweight championship in 1947, the world championship title eluded him in his three attempts to win the belt from arch-nemesis Ike Williams.

The career highlight for Carlos Chavez, "The Iron Man," was a 12-round unanimous decision win over Manuel Ortiz for the California featherweight championship on October 22, 1946, at the Olympic Auditorium. Chavez, no relation to boxer Fabela Chavez, was from the Palo Verde neighborhood of Chavez Ravine (a place known as the "Poor Man's Shangri-La"). Chavez retired with a record of 69 victories (20 knockouts), 37 losses, and 10 draws while fighting from 1939 to 1956.

"Fabulous" Fabela Chavez was a relentless punching featherweight boxer from the Bunker Hill district next to downtown Los Angeles. Chavez won the California featherweight championship by a 12-round split decision victory over Lauro Salas at Hollywood Legion Stadium on July 27, 1951. Chavez, a Roosevelt High alumnus, was managed by George Parnassus and trained by Johnny Villaflor while fighting from 1945 to 1955. Chavez ended with a record of 47 wins (15 knockouts), 24 losses, and 5 draws.

The two top Mexican American boxing idols of the decade met once in the ring. In a featherweight dustup, Manuel Ortiz dealt a TKO loss to Enrique Bolanos at the Olympic Auditorium on August 29, 1944. Bolanos's corner threw in the towel after he was knocked down for the second time in the sixth heat. Looking like a doo-wop singing group, from left to right, are Joe Herrera (actor/promoter), Bolanos, Ortiz, and unidentified. (Courtesy of Bob Recendez.)

Manager George Parnassus (right) meets with West Coast swing-era boxer of the 1940s Enrique Bolanos at the Alexandria Hotel. A strong bond existed between Mexican fight fans and Parnassus because he understood their "fierce national pride," loyalty, and friendship. Parnassus was a genius in promoting the smaller fighters. With his strong connections to the Mexican people, he realized bigger gates than the heavyweight fighters of the time were bringing in. Bolanos spoke of Parnassus to the *Los Angeles Times*: "He's a great man to me. A good matchmaker, a good father and a good friend. When I was fighting, he was like a father to me, too. He took care of me, even put me to bed. But, still, I didn't take care of myself. Now, when I do, it doesn't matter. But he was right." Below, Bolanos gets his hands wrapped by trainer Johnny Villaflor.

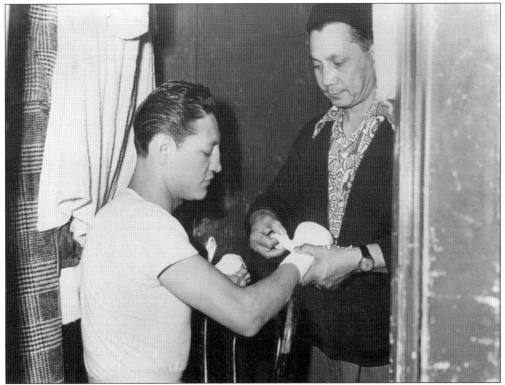

Enrique Bolanos (second from left) and stablemate Fabela Chavez (second from right) hang out with friends (unidentified) at the gym in 1947. George Parnassus, manager of both fighters, recalled to the *Los Angeles Times*, "Bolanos would have been a great champion, but he had one fault. He couldn't say no to his so-called friends. If he had taken care of himself, he would have been the greatest. People cheered him even when he missed a punch."

In May 1946, Enrique Bolanos (center) proposed to a radiant Ruby Gallegos (left) at Mike's Tailor Shop on Third Street in downtown Los Angeles, with Mike ? looking on. Ruby told the *Los Angeles Times*, "Enrique's dream—his whole purpose in life—was to be champion of the world. He was groomed for it. When it didn't happen after the third fight [with Ike Williams], he lost his spirit. It was very sad. And his heart truly wasn't in it again."

Luis Magana (left) looks over photographs with Gabriel Hap Navarro (right) and lightweight left-hooking specialist Enrique Bolanos (center) during the 1940s. Magana was the Spanish publicist for the Olympic Auditorium from the late 1930s to 1984. Navarro was assistant matchmaker to Cal Working at Hollywood Legion Stadium from 1948 to 1953, then became the head matchmaker there from 1953 to 1955, until Jackie Leonard suddenly took over the position.

In their first duke on June 3, 1947, "The Durango Dropper" Enrique Bolanos scored a seventh-round TKO over tough-nosed veteran "Gentleman" John Thomas (of Central Avenue in Los Angeles) to capture the California lightweight championship in front of a full house at Wrigley Field. In the image, Bolanos (left) ices Thomas in the fourth round of their rematch at the Olympic Auditorium with 10,400 screaming fans in attendance on September 30, 1947. Thomas would retire from the ring after this fight.

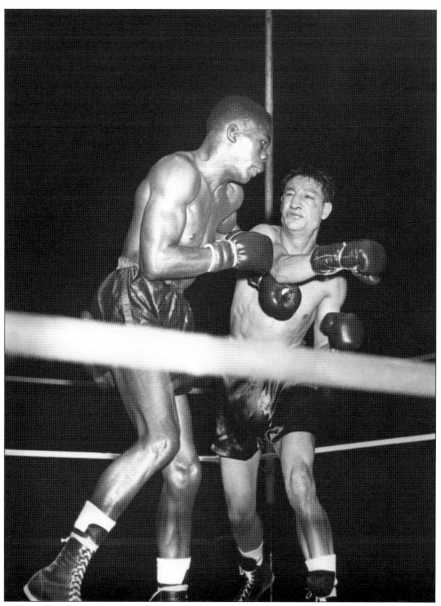

Boxing journalist Johnny Ortiz told David A. Avila of the Sweet Science website that "Enrique Bolanos had the greatest footwork I have ever seen or will ever see, he and Sugar Ray Robinson. Los Angeles fight fans were crazy about him, there was something about him that was kind of mesmerizing. He always fought before sell-out crowds." Bolanos slams a hard right to the head of lightweight champion Ike Williams (left), of Trenton, New Jersey, in their May 25, 1948, bout at Wrigley Field (the second meeting in their trilogy). Though "The Durango Kid" Bolanos was the aggressor that night, Williams retained the title in a thrilling but disputed 15-round split decision. "Many people say that Enrique won the second fight with Williams," remembered Luis Magana, publicist for the Olympic Auditorium. Johnny Ortiz reminisced, "After he [Bolanos] lost . . . his three fights with the great Ike Williams, he kind of lost interest, he was just never the same. His days as a serious contender were over for the most part. He began drinking, putting an end to a once brilliant career."

Boxing writer Bert Sugar called Manuel Ortiz "a breakthrough Latino champion. This longtime champ was an all-around slick fighter, the forerunner of the West Coast Latino fighter. . . . The first great American-born Latino fighter had been Ortiz, who ruled the bantamweight roost from 1942 to 1950, with one short two-month hiatus." Matchmaker Hap Navarro also praised "The El Centro Destroyer" as "a master boxer who could lure an opponent into fierce exchanges which he usually won." World bantamweight champion Ortiz jumps rope at Oquinarenne Gym in Paris, France, getting ready for his nontitle bout against hometown boxer Theo Medina. Below, Ortiz knocks Medina to the canvas en route to a 10-round decision at the Palais des Sports in Paris on November 14, 1949. In addition to his world championship belt, Ortiz also won the California bantamweight title in 1942 and the Orient featherweight title in 1951.

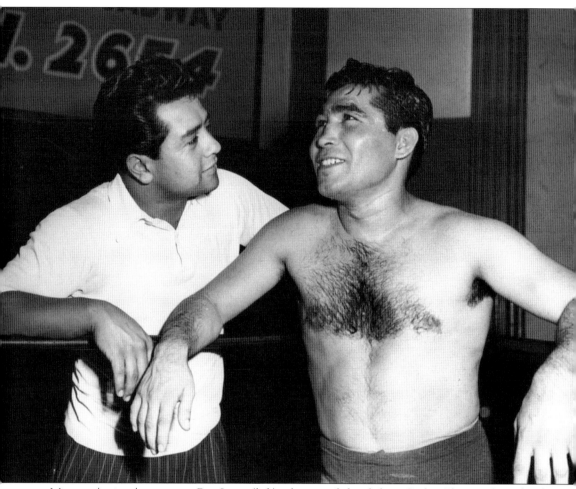

Manager/trainer/cornerman Ray Luna (left) relaxes with his fighter Carlos Chavez after a hard workout at the Moose Gym in Los Angeles in 1948. Luna also worked with boxers Art Aragon, Keeny Teran, and Manuel Ortiz—all towards the end of their careers. Luna appears with Aragon in a dressing-room scene in *The Ring*, a 1952 movie that chronicles the struggles of a young Mexican American boxer in Los Angeles as he rises in the fight game. Chavez would defeat "Golden Boy" Aragon by a 10-round unanimous decision on June 6, 1950, at the Olympic Auditorium, setting the stage for a rematch. But their second fight was hardly a struggle, as Aragon knocked out Chavez in the very first round on November 21, 1950, also at the Olympic. This outcome produced much skepticism, as Chavez had never been counted out in his long career. Chavez eventually testified before a California investigating committee that he did take a one-round dive against Aragon. Chavez was sick from loss of blood due to hemorrhoids and stated, "there was no use in getting hurt." Aragon told the *Los Angeles Times*, "He was a slow starter, but later on he would kill you. Carlos was not a bully, and I liked him for that. He was a classy guy. He was one of the few guys in boxing history I looked up to."

Three

THE 1950s
WHEN THE LITTLE GUYS WERE KINGS

You know what I remember even more than my fights with all the boos . . . was the nights I'd go to the Olympic with some broad, just to watch a fight. Remember, in those days, I owned this town. It was just me and the Rams then. And all I had to do was just walk down the aisle to my seat. Right away, the boos would start coming down from the balcony. By the time I'd reach my seat, they'd have to stop the fight until everyone settled down. The entire crowd would be on its feet booing. I loved it. I do miss that.

—Art Aragon, as told to Earl Gustkey, *Los Angeles Times*

If Manuel Ortiz and Enrique Bolanos were the rulers of Mexican American boxing in the 1940s, then "Golden Boy" Art Aragon was the king of Los Angeles during the 1950s. Though supremely talented, Aragon never captured the lightweight crown as only one world champion existed in each weight class, making a title belt difficult to obtain.

The "little guys" were popular because they were nonstop punchers. Boxers were wild and wonderful as *the golden age* continued. On New Year's Eve 1951, Aragon went to the Sunset (a cocktail bar in Echo Park) and saw fellow rival lightweight boxer Lauro Salas. A drunken brawl ensued, and police were called in. Aragon recounted to the *Los Angeles Times*, "I walked in and he said, 'Arturo, mi amigo' . . . I said get away from me, you ugly _ _ _! He was there with two gorgeous (women) and I guess that (ticked) me off. Then I took a punch at him, and damn it, I missed. Big mistake. Never miss a little guy. He was so small, I couldn't find him." Observers say Salas won the scuffle.

Aragon courted such Hollywood A-list starlets of the day as Marilyn Monroe, Jayne Mansfield, and Mamie Van Doren. "The Golden Boy was the perfect title for him," Van Doren told the *Los Angeles Times*, "His smile turned everyone on. His skin was golden. His floppy hair bounced so perfectly. He was just so sexy."

"Golden Boy" Art Aragon was the biggest box-office draw for boxing in Los Angeles during the 1950s. Growing up in Boyle Heights, he attended Roosevelt High School before going on to an illustrious career as a top-ranked lightweight and welterweight contender. Entering the ring with royal swagger, Aragon entertained and fought to standing room only crowds at the Olympic Auditorium, Wrigley Field, and Hollywood Legion Stadium.

Bantamweight champion Manuel Ortiz, in his 23rd (and final) world title bout, traveled all the way to Wembley Stadium in Johannesburg, South Africa, to face 22-year-old local contender Vic Toweel (13-0) on May 31, 1950. In front of 20,000 spectators, the quicker challenger Toweel sustained a broken nose and cut left ear, but still pulled off a 15-round decision victory over the 33-year-old titleholder, taking the belt Ortiz held for eight long years.

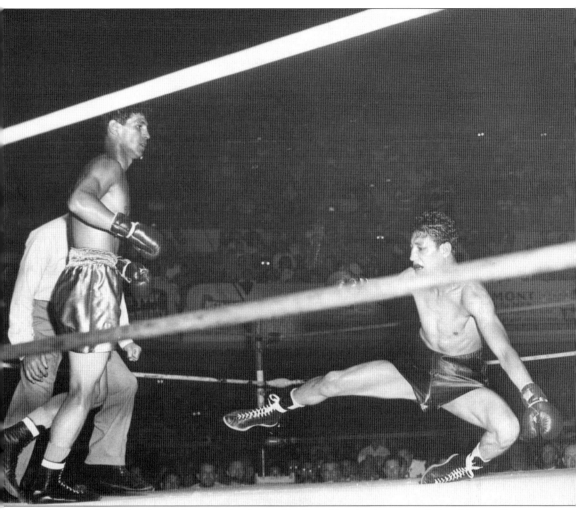

At 22 years of age, Art Aragon's stature in the world of local boxing lore grew during his two-fight rivalry with Enrique Bolanos at the Olympic Auditorium. Aragon recalled to the *Los Angeles Times*, "Bolanos was an idol to the Mexican community in Los Angeles. He was a really good fighter, too, and he was an idol of mine when I was coming up. But I beat him bad twice, and they didn't like that. I didn't like it much, either. But then I started noticing that the more people hated me, the more they'd pay top dollar to come boo me." In the passing of the torch, Aragon (left) TKO'd a still young 25-year-old Bolanos in the 12th round on Valentine's Day, 1950. This was the making of the "Golden Boy." In the rematch a few months later on July 18, Aragon floored Bolanos again by TKO in the third round. After this, the boos began to get louder for "Golden Boy" Aragon. As Olympic matchmaker Don Chargin remembered, "Mexican fans didn't forgive Aragon for knocking out Bolanos."

A well-behaved, well-dressed crowd observes referee Mushy Callahan (at top) rushing in as Art Aragon drops lightweight switch-hitting Mario Trigo ("The Spoiler" or "The Upset Kid") during their draw at the Olympic Auditorium on December 12, 1950. The huskily built warhorse Trigo, of Monterrey, Nuevo León, Mexico, was based out of Los Angeles as he fought the best West Coast prizefighters of the day, ending with 68 wins (15 knockouts), 47 losses, and 11 draws.

A triumphant Art Aragon lays his head on the ropes and weeps tears of joy after ring announcer Jimmy Lennon (far left) called his 10-round split decision victory over world lightweight champion Jimmy Carter in a nontitle bout at the Olympic Auditorium on August 28, 1951. As Carter (top left) gets his eye worked on, Jimmy Roche, Aragon's manager (far right), and Willie Ketchum, Carter's manager, indulge in a heated argument.

Keeny Teran (born Ignacio Teran) was a promising, baby-faced flyweight boxer from Boyle Heights. Keeny (slang for "The Little One") started off as a local teenage boxing sensation during the Pachuco era, but was later plagued by a narcotics addiction that followed him all his life. Boxing manager Frank "kiki" Baltazar Sr. recalled, "Keeny was a small guy who at the age of 18 looked like he was 14 years old or younger. But if you tried to take advantage of his youthful looks in the ring, he would make sure you paid for it." On June 22, 1951, two of Los Angeles' hottest bantamweight prospects—Keeny Teran (6-0) and Gil Cadilli (7-1-1)—met in the semi-windup at the Hollywood Legion Stadium Fight For Life benefit for the City of Hope (a cancer-treatment hospital). These crosstown rivals fought their hearts out in one of the greatest six-rounders in California boxing history, with the bout ending in a suspenseful draw. Credit goes out to assistant matchmaker Hap Navarro for making this fight happen on the undercard of the Enrique Bolanos–Eddie Chavez scrap.

Keeny Teran (right) hits the heavy bag at the Moose Gym in Los Angeles with assistance from manager Ray Luna (left) in the mid-1950s. Early in his career, Teran trained at the Teamsters Gym and Main St. Gym, both in downtown Los Angeles, while managed by "Senator" Johnny Forbes. Women loved and opponents feared the speedy Teran, who began his career in 1951 by going 12-0-1 with 7 knockouts, earning him the trophy as the Olympic Auditorium "Fighter of the Year." A notable bout for Keeny was a six-round split decision win over rugged Tommy Umeda of Hawaii on August 21, 1951, at the Olympic Auditorium. But in their third bout, Teran fell victim to a savage beating by Umeda, resulting in a seventh-round TKO for his first defeat, on June 24, 1952 (also at the Olympic). On the eve of Teran's comeback for the fourth and final Umeda fight, *Los Angeles Mirror* reporter Lou Larkin broke the story of Teran's heroin addiction in his page one article, making Keeny angry, ashamed, and confused by the public disclosure.

A reason for the huge popularity of "Golden Boy" Art Aragon during the early 1950s was because he was the only *game* in town (other than the Los Angeles Rams), as the Dodgers, Angels, and Lakers had not yet arrived. Though Aragon beat many of the best opponents around, the world title belt would prove elusive. In a storied 116-fight career that lasted from 1944 to 1960, Aragon's bout vs. lightweight champion Jimmy Carter, of Bronx, New York, on November 14, 1951, would be his one and only attempt at the crown. Below, in the opening heat, Aragon catches a left jab from Carter (right) in a sign this rematch would be much different than their first go-round. Aragon, weakened from having to make weight, was dropped to the canvas in the sixth and 15th rounds as Carter retained his title with a 15-round unanimous decision at the Olympic Auditorium.

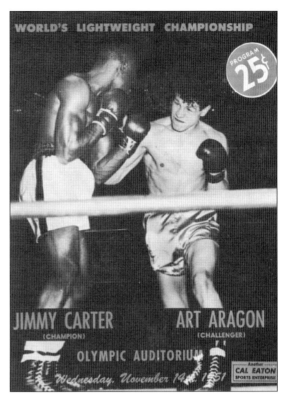

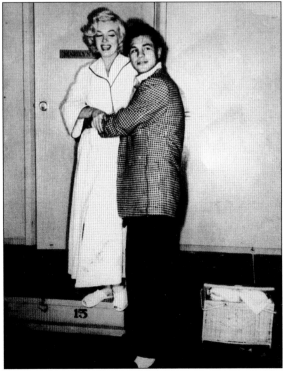

The Mexican Sportswriters Association held its first banquet at Club Zarape, at 2905 Sunset Boulevard, Los Angeles, on November 25, 1951, to present the award to the most outstanding Mexican fighter of all time. Tallies were done through popular voting in the Spanish-language newspaper *La Opinion*. Hap Navarro emceed the event, and receiving trophies are, from left to right, Bert Colima, Art Aragon, "Baby" Arizmendi, Manuel Ortiz, and winner Enrique Bolanos.

As always, "Golden Boy" Art Aragon kept company in the arms of beautiful women. In the image, Aragon (right) visits actress Marilyn Monroe on a movie set in the early 1950s. As Aragon so eloquently told Earl Gustkey, *Los Angeles Times* staff writer, "Hey, in those days, I didn't drink with bums, pal."

Keeny Teran's fourth fight with Tommy Umeda was one of the most courageous comeback stories in the history of the ring. With Teran's lifelong drug addiction now exposed by the press, "The Problem Child of the Ring" survived a broken nose, sprained left hand, and a sixth-round knockdown to win a dramatic 10-round unanimous decision over his rival Umeda in front of 6,500 rooting fans at the Olympic Auditorium on December 9, 1952. After the fight, all of Hollywood came knocking on his door to do his life story. Teran then won the North American flyweight title on February 5, 1955, by beating Johnny Ortega of Oakland in a 10th-round TKO at Hollywood Legion Stadium. But tragically, Keeny's drug problems dimmed his once bright future, as Frank "kiki" Baltazar Sr. recalled, "As a boxer, Keeny Teran mostly battled his own demons, denying himself a chance to fight for the world title." Teran fought from 1951 to 1955 (retiring at the tender age of 23) and left boxing with a record of 25 wins (14 knockouts), 4 losses, and 1 draw.

Lauro Salas, "The Little Lion of Monterrey," Nuevo León, Mexico, was a bighearted brawler who was not afraid to fight anyone. Salas rejoices after dethroning Jimmy Carter in a slugfest to become the new lightweight champion of the world by a 15-round split decision on May 14, 1952, at the Olympic Auditorium. The wild-living Salas was a colorful Los Angeles boxing figure who fought from 1946 to 1961, ending with 91 wins (45 knockouts), 58 losses, and 13 draws.

The defining moment of California featherweight/bantamweight champion Gil Cadilli's ring career came when he defeated Willie Pep, one of boxing's all-time greats, in a nontitle bout on March 30, 1955. Cadilli (right) opened up a cut on Pep's right eyebrow in the fourth round on his way to a 10-round split decision victory at Parks Air Force Base in California. Featherweight kingpin Pep was an incredible 188-6-1 before this bout.

Manager Sid Flaherty (left) oversees "L.A.'s Featherweight Hope" Gil Cadilli's workout on the heavy bag at the New Garden Gym in Boston for his upcoming battle against No. 2–ranked Miguel Berrios of Puerto Rico. Cadilli went on to upset Berrios in a 10-round split decision at the Mechanics Building in Boston, Massachusetts, on January 16, 1957. Cadilli ended his career with a record of 31 wins (10 knockouts), 25 losses, and 7 draws while fighting from 1950 to 1963.

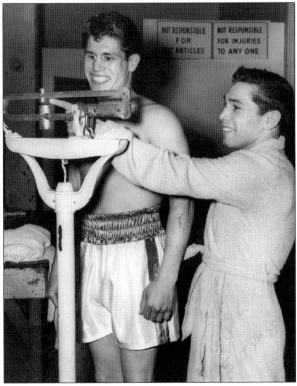

Vince Delgado was a featherweight from the Palo Verde neighborhood of Chavez Ravine and nephew of boxer Carlos Chavez. At the Main St. Gym, Delgado (right) checks the weight of opponent Alfredo Escobar of Redondo Beach, whom he defeated in 1957 (majority decision 10) and 1958 (split decision 10), both at Hollywood Legion Stadium. Delgado, managed by Gig Rooney and "Senator" Johnny Forbes, fought from 1952 to 1960, retiring with 16 wins (7 knockouts), 8 losses, and 2 draws. (Courtesy of Bob Recendez.)

Through local televised bouts, Art Aragon's star began to rise, going a perfect 13-0 while fighting at Hollywood Legion Stadium in 1949. Johnny Allen, boxing editor of the *Los Angeles Daily News*, ran a story that read, "Hollywood Legion had found its Golden Boy in Art Aragon." This inspired Hollywood Legion Stadium assistant matchmaker Hap Navarro to contact head publicist Jimmy O'Toole of Columbia Pictures Studios in Hollywood to arrange a prefight ceremony at the Legion in which actor William Holden, who starred in the 1939 boxing movie *Golden Boy*, would pin the "Golden Boy" moniker on his friend Aragon. The colorful Aragon entered the ring wearing gold trunks and a gold robe, becoming "The Bad Boy of Boxing" for his trash-talking and nightclubbing exploits. A glum-faced Aragon (left) walks with first wife, Georgina, after being indicted on a felony charge by a Los Angeles grand jury on February 21, 1957. He was accused of offering welterweight Dick Goldstein a $500 bribe to take a dive in a fight that never happened. The supposed bout was to have taken place in San Antonio, Texas, in December 1956 but was canceled when Aragon became ill with fever. Aragon denied the charge, insisting he told Goldstein that "if he was smart, he shouldn't get up if he went down . . . to avoid further punishment." Aragon told the *Los Angeles Times*, "When the appellate court threw out the conviction, my attorney [Paul Caruso] was out of town. I wired him 'Justice has triumphed!' He wired back: 'Appeal at once.'"

Rudy Jordan was a southpaw lightweight boxer from Los Angeles who fought from 1952 to 1958. Managed and trained by Howie Steindler, Jordan finished with a record of 22 victories (5 knockouts), 7 losses, and 3 draws. Jordan's most memorable victory was a six-round TKO over fading ex-lightweight champion Jimmy Carter (left) at Fresno Memorial Auditorium on September 23, 1958 (stoppage occurring due to bad cuts under Carter's left eye).

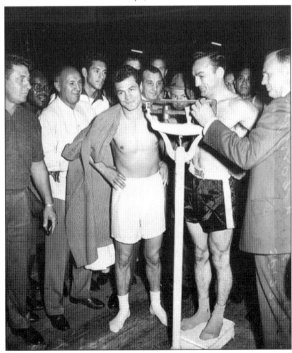

Art Aragon (white shorts) looks away as Carmen Basilio tips the scale and assistant secretary Clayton Frye (far right) of the California State Athletic Commission supervises the weigh-in for their bout at Wrigley Field on September 5, 1958. During the weigh-in, former welterweight and middleweight champion Basilio innocently asked Aragon, "How you doing?" to which Aragon replied, "Not so good. Both my wife and my girlfriend are here."

Carmen Basilio throws a left jab at Art Aragon (right) on his way to a TKO victory on September 5, 1958, outdoors at Wrigley Field, located at Forty-second Street and Avalon Boulevard in South Central Los Angeles. Basilio, "The Upstate Onion Farmer" from Canastota, New York, was unleashing such a relentless attack that referee Tommy Hart came to Aragon's corner and said, "Son, I'm close to stopping the bout," to which Aragon replied, "What are you waiting for?" Aragon's corner had no choice but to throw in the towel during the eighth round, as Basilio brutally broke down Aragon piece by piece during the match. Aragon would say, "My biggest purse was $87,000 for the Basilio fight, but after he got through it cost me $92,000 to get out of the hospital." Aragon's wonderful wit continued. When asked, "Would you consider a rematch with Basilio?" he replied, "Only if I can take in a .45 with me." A headline later appeared in the newspapers about his first divorce, which read, "Wife sues Aragon, Names 15 Women!" "She missed three," said Aragon.

Cocky, arrogant, and talented, Art Aragon had a love-hate relationship with the audience. He knew how to play the villain role perfectly, thumbing his nose at fans from the ring. The plan worked so well that he had them right in the palm of his hand: the Olympic Auditorium would be sold out for his next fight. He was the California lightweight champion, the unofficial Olympic Auditorium box-office champion, an actor, a flamboyant character who counted celebrities as friends, and married four times. Boxing fan Richard Orozco recalls, "Art Aragon was an early version of Muhammad Ali, he was way ahead of his time. As well as a great left hook, he was a great self-promoter who would negotiate his own contracts." Aragon left boxing with a record of 90 wins (62 knockouts), 20 losses, 6 draws and was never knocked out by a 10-count. He told the *Los Angeles Times*, "I quit too late. I fought one year longer than I should have. I always said I'd get out when I lost two in a row. Seemed like after I'd lose one, I'd get lucky and win."

In their first bout, Compton native Cisco Andrade dropped a 10-round split decision to the smaller but gutsy Lauro Salas of Mexico at the Olympic Auditorium on February 17, 1955. Local contender Andrade then took the next two bouts over former world lightweight champion Salas. Andrade, in his only bid for the lightweight title, lost a lopsided decision to world champion Joe Brown of Houston, Texas, on October 28, 1960, at the Olympic.

Danny Valdez, "The Pride of East Los Angeles," was a crowd-pleasing featherweight boxer from the tough Eastside neighborhood Maravilla. Valdez (in robe) gets his gloves taken off by manager Art Arvizu (left) after winning the California featherweight title over Dwight Hawkins on October 1, 1959, at the Olympic Auditorium. Cornerman Tio Serrano crouches to pick up coins thrown into the ring by fans showing their appreciation after an exciting fight. (Photograph by John G. Lopez.)

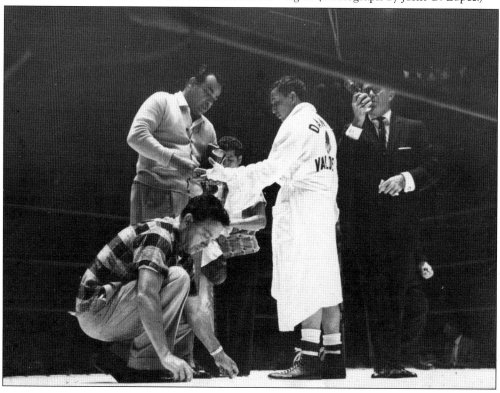

Four

THE 1960s
"WAR-A-WEEK" AT THE CORNER OF EIGHTEENTH AND GRAND

Mando Ramos . . . a teen-age phenom who has everything—looks, personality and great natural talent. He's the Elvis Presley of the boxing ring.

—Sid Ziff, *Los Angeles Times* sports columnist, June 2, 1967

Lightweight Mando Ramos held court at the Olympic Auditorium, becoming the darling of promoter Aileen Eaton. Twenty-seven of his 49 total bouts were held at the Olympic (the shrine of Los Angeles boxing). Ted Sares writes in "Los Vatos of Southern California":

> There was something special about him, he was able to connect with and capture the hearts of Mexican American boxing like few others. Ramos became one of the greatest sports stars in Los Angeles. Lopez and Chacon and even Aragon before them were tremendous box-office attractions, but what was really incredible was that by the age of eighteen, Mando virtually owned the Olympic.

Ramos became the youngest man in history ever to win the lightweight title, but life in the fast lane took it away just as quickly. Things came too easy for Ramos: fame, good looks, charisma, and natural boxing ability. Winning the title only provided fuel for the mischievous angel of Long Beach. He told Jack Hirsch of *Boxing News*, "I celebrated until the end of my career," and said to the *Los Angeles Times*, "I sold out the Olympic Auditorium in my ninth fight. Money was everywhere . . . I was 19, 20. What did I know? By 1974, I was sleeping in cars."

From 1964 to 1984, Don "War-a-Week" Chargin was the matchmaker at the Olympic Auditorium, located on the corner of Eighteenth Street and Grand Avenue in downtown Los Angeles. Most of those years, he worked under promoter Aileen Eaton, then later for Rogelio Robles. The Olympic was the epicenter for Thursday night fights, as local television broadcaster Jim Healy kept things buzzing with excitement: "It's allllll ooooover!" In fact, it was Healy who christened Chargin with the nickname "War-a-Week" because he was such a busy matchmaker. Chargin and his wife, Lorraine, were essential to the survival of the Olympic, the last weekly fight club in America.

After retirement, "Golden Boy" Art Aragon went into the bail bonds business in downtown Los Angeles, and his motto was "I'll Get You Out, If It Takes 10 Years."

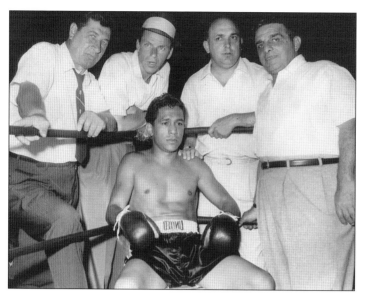

Cisco Andrade was a homegrown, classic-style lightweight boxer known as "The Compton Comet." Fighting from 1952 to 1962, Andrade posted a career record of 46 victories (26 knockouts), 12 losses, and 1 draw. In his corner are, from left to right, Al Silvani (trainer/ actor), Frank Sinatra (singer/actor/ comanager of Andrade), Andrade, Hank Sanicola (manager of Sinatra), and Ralph Gambina (comanager of Andrade).

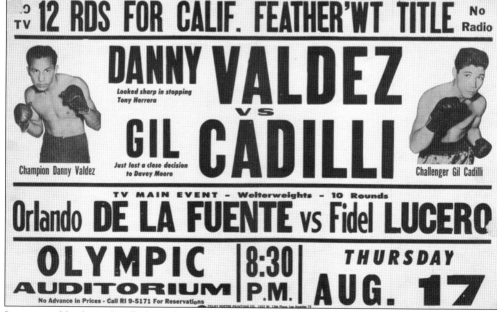

In a natural-built rivalry, flashy Gil Cadilli (Roosevelt High), from "Los Flats" in Boyle Heights, and scrappy Danny Valdez (Garfield High), from Maravilla, fought twice at the Olympic Auditorium. In their first meeting (poster depicted), Cadilli took the California featherweight title from Valdez by 12-round split decision on August 17, 1961. In an immediate nontitle rematch, Valdez won a 10-round unanimous decision over Cadilli on September 21, 1961.

Raul Rojas, from San Pedro, rose from being a gang member to featherweight champion of the world in 1968. Growing up in Watts and East Los Angeles, Rojas recounted to the *Los Angeles Times*, "All I ever was, was tough. I thought I'd put it to work. If it were not for boxing, I'd probably either be in San Quentin or would already have made the trip to the gas chamber."

Danny Valdez receives a visit from Garfield High School sweetheart and wife, Dolores (Sanchez), at the Main St. Gym. The newlyweds pose while Valdez was in training for Javier "Sugar" Zatarain of Mexico, who Valdez knocked out in the ninth round at the Olympic Auditorium on August 13, 1964. Valdez fought from 1957 to 1966, ending with a record of 31 wins (14 knockouts) and 12 losses. (Courtesy of Danny Valdez.)

Ernie Lopez poses with his wife, Marcia, at the Main St. Gym office in May 1966. After Lopez's two failed title fights with Jose "Mantequilla" Napoles, Marcia (Park) Lopez recalled, "I think he lost confidence; his goal was destroyed. He was depressed and angry. We started having marital problems." Younger brother Danny Lopez remembered, "It was the losses to Napoles and the divorce that sent Ernie into a tailspin. He was a hurt man."

On his way to the world title, Rodolfo "El Gato" Gonzalez (left) scored two wins (decision 6; TKO 4) in 1966 over Ray Coleman (right) of Phoenix, Arizona, at the Fremont Hotel in Las Vegas. Assisting the two boxers in the promotion is glamorous actress Jayne Mansfield. "El Gato" (active from 1959 to 1974) is not to be confused with the Mexico City lightweight contender of the same name, Rodolfo "Gato" Gonzalez (active from 1978 to 2004).

Mando Ramos, Lightweight Champion

Mando Ramos from Long Beach, California, was a shooting star in the lightweight division. With so much natural boxing talent, he was fighting the main event at the Olympic Auditorium in only his eighth professional bout. Ramos remembered that as an eight-year-old boy, he used to ride to the Olympic Auditorium with his father, Ray. He told the *Los Angeles Times*, "I used to sit back in the bleachers and dream about filling that place up, and later I did." At 20 years of age, Ramos became the youngest boxer in history to win the lightweight championship of the world when he defeated Carlos Teo Cruz, of the Dominican Republic, by an 11th-round TKO at the Los Angeles Memorial Coliseum on February 18, 1969. Chicano icon Ramos is immortalized in the 1992 Universal Pictures film *American Me* (starring Edward James Olmos) when East Los Angeles gang members talk boxing: "The greatest fighter pound-for-pound, *vatos*? See, without a doubt, *con los* left jabs, *los* hooks, *los* uppercuts . . . y *toda la Madre*, hands down . . . Mando Ramos."

Mando Ramos grew up quickly in front of a vast Southern California television viewing audience during the 1960s. Rich Roberts of the *Los Angeles Times* called Ramos "a wide-eyed assassin on spindly legs, he could rip off combinations like a machine gun, slip punches like a fencing master, render an opponent senseless with either hand and then dance the rest of the night away. Life was an endless party, and the party was wherever Ramos happened to be. Many nights, it was the Olympic Auditorium which he filled to the rafters. Like Art Aragon before him and a succession of hard-fighting Latins after him, Ramos had his era in L.A. boxing, too." In this image, teenage whiz kid Ramos (center) keeps veteran southpaw Jorge "Baby" Salazar (right) of Mexico City against the ropes as referee John Thomas (left) observes the action. Ramos remained undefeated in his 11th professional fight with a 10-round unanimous decision win over Salazar at the Olympic Auditorium on September 8, 1966. (Photograph by Paul M. Orduna.)

Mando Ramos, who was tall for a lightweight, had the looks of a Latin matinee idol, which drew many female fans to his fights at the Olympic Auditorium. Ramos played escort to numerous Hollywood lovelies, and here he is seen leaving the Olympic with a friend named "Bunnie" during the late 1960s. (Photograph by Paul M. Orduna.)

Ruben Navarro, "The Maravilla Kid," got his nickname from the hardscrabble East L.A. housing projects where he was raised. A top lightweight contender, he ended with a record of 33 wins (15 knockouts), 8 losses, and 2 draws while fighting from 1967 to 1974. Navarro loved the nightlife as much as boxing. "I had everything a guy could want . . . booze, broads, anything money could buy," he told the *Los Angeles Herald Examiner*.

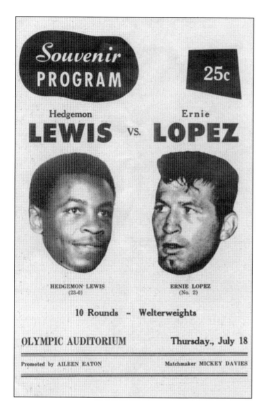

Souvenir PROGRAM 25c

Hedgemon
LEWIS VS. **LOPEZ** Ernie

HEDGEMON LEWIS
(23-0)

ERNIE LOPEZ
(No. 2)

10 Rounds – Welterweights

OLYMPIC AUDITORIUM   Thursday., July 18

Promoted by AILEEN EATON   Matchmaker MICKEY DAVIES

Top welterweight contenders Ernie "Indian Red" Lopez of Arcadia and Hedgemon Lewis of Los Angeles, by way of Detroit, engaged in a three-fight battle. Boxing writers call Lopez's two victories over Lewis the best showings of his career. In the program on the left from their first fight on July 18, 1968, the fierce-hitting Lopez knocked out an undefeated Lewis (23-0) in the ninth round in front of a sold-out crowd of 10,400 at the Olympic Auditorium. Lopez, who won the California welterweight championship in 1967, was nicknamed "Indian Red" because of his red hair and Native American heritage that was mixed with Mexican and Irish blood. Pictured below are, from left to right, Lewis, future world lightweight champion Mando Ramos, and Lopez. Lopez fought from 1963 until an ill-advised on the spot comeback in 1987, ending his career with 48 wins (24 knockouts), 13 losses, and 1 draw.

Mando Ramos was a colorful and charismatic boxer with a killer instinct who fought to many turn away crowds at the Olympic Auditorium. He drew celebrities to his fights, such as John Wayne, Kirk Douglas, Elizabeth Taylor, Bill Cosby, and Connie Stevens. Ramos (right) is seen standing next to comedian Richard Pryor at the Olympic Auditorium in 1966. (Photograph by Paul M. Orduna.)

Besides battling opponents in the ring from 1963 to 1970, Raul Rojas had to fight his own personal demons like drugs and alcohol. Known as one of the original bad boys of local boxing lore, Rojas (right) ironically gives advice to Los Angeles Chief of Police Thomas Reddin in 1968. Rojas was comanaged by Jackie McCoy and Lee Prlia and finished with 38 wins (24 knockouts), 7 losses, and 2 draws.

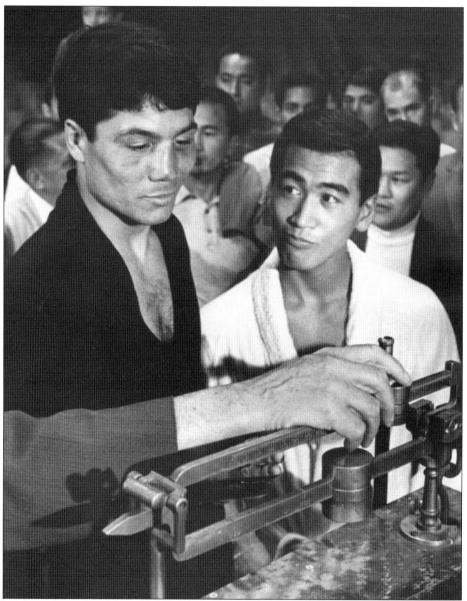

A highlight of Raul Rojas's career was his back-to-back victories over Mexican sensational knockout artist Ricardo "Pajarito" Moreno. In their first fight, Rojas won by TKO in the third round at the Olympic Auditorium on March 17, 1966, and in the following match, Rojas scored a second-round knockout over Moreno at the Los Angeles Sports Arena on June 3, 1966. Little Raul Rojas walked the streets of San Pedro like a giant after defeating Enrique Higgins of Colombia for the vacant WBA featherweight title by a 15-round unanimous decision at the Olympic Auditorium on March 28, 1968. In this image, the face of Rojas (left) appears slightly bruised as he tips the scale at the weigh-in for the first defense of his 126-pound belt against Shozo Saijo (right) of Japan, who only three months earlier beat an out-of-shape Rojas in a nontitle fight at the Olympic Auditorium. Rojas's stay as world champion would last only six months, as he lost his title to Saijo by a 15-round unanimous decision at the Los Angeles Memorial Coliseum on September 27, 1968.

Ruben Navarro, "The Maravilla Kid," begins the lonely walk to the ring at the Forum, where he lost a 12-round unanimous decision to Arturo Lomeli of Guadalajara, Jalisco, Mexico, in a world lightweight title elimination bout held on November 4, 1968. In a 1970 rematch, Navarro went the distance for a 12-round split decision over Lomeli at the Olympic Auditorium, earning him the vacant North American Boxing Federation lightweight title. (Photograph by George Rodriguez.)

Promoter extraordinaire George Parnassus (left) talks strategy at ringside during his November 4, 1968, card at the Inglewood Forum featuring Jose "Mantequilla" Napoles. While employed at the Forum, the shrewd 73-year-old, white-haired Parnassus staged more title bouts than any man in history and brought in the biggest gates ever seen in California. Parnassus told *West Magazine*, "I like to see good boxers make money." (Photograph by George Rodriguez.)

George Parnassus, "The Golden Greek," became matchmaker at the Olympic Auditorium in 1957 (under promoter Cal Eaton) and, within a year, the Olympic experienced sharp increases at the gate due to his understanding that smaller weight classes were huge attractions to the blossoming Mexican American population. Parnassus was revered by many in the Latino community. "They [Mexicans] are brave, gentle people who deeply love their families and children," Parnassus told *West Magazine*, "They are proud and they understand friendship. They are the best friends in the world." By 1967, Parnassus had moved down the 110 Freeway to the brand-new Fabulous Forum to begin another successful stint as promoter (under owner Jack Kent Cooke). Parnassus is pictured at his second-floor headquarters at the Alexandria Hotel, called "The Waldorf of the West," where he is protected by "golden-haired angels with glowing pink faces." Visiting boxers and celebrities from Mexico stayed at the Alexandria, located on the corner of Fifth and Spring in downtown Los Angeles. Parnassus is captured in 1969 by the masterful lens of photographer George Rodriguez (using his Canon camera).

By the shade of the 10 Freeway, on the corner of Eighteenth and Grand, lies the Olympic Auditorium, a monument to the glory days of boxing in Los Angeles. Nostalgic Angelenos still fondly recall the oft-repeated phone number of the Olympic Auditorium, Richmond 9-5171, which has been etched into pop-culture posterity. Local fight fans, inspired by the rise of Mexican American fighters, rallied around their fistic heroes at this downtown cathedral of boxing, which was originally built in 1925 to showcase the 1932 Los Angeles Olympic Games. Longtime Spanish-language publicist Luis Magana told the *Los Angeles Times*, "The Olympic was the cradle of Mexican idols. In the years that I worked there, I have seen young fighters walk through those doors loaded with dreams and plans and illusions and I've seen them walk out as idols, as world champions." Don Chargin, matchmaker, told the *Los Angeles Times*, "It was the place. It was the Madison Square Garden of the West." Chargin explained how business took place at the Olympic: "It's the same thing we've always done. It's the format Mrs. Eaton developed. You find talent, steer them into a title fight. Make your money off that big one." On the evening of a title fight, the Olympic Auditorium carried a special magic, violent, and electric atmosphere that permeated the entire arena. (Photograph by Theo Ehret 1969.)

Mando Ramos (center), shown dancing with two showgirls, enjoyed the nightlife and all that the late 1960s had to offer a talented young boxer in Southern California. But with everything coming so easy (including big paydays that made Ramos the richest teenager in sports), wine, women, and song took it away just as fast. Ramos displayed respectable knockout power but abused his boxing potential by living in the fast lane. Boxing historian and former fighter Rick Farris said, "Mando Ramos had a gift, but he also had a curse." Rich Roberts of the *Los Angeles Times* wrote, "He owned the late '60s and early '70s. He won and lost the lightweight title twice, before titles were split so many ways they looked like leftover pizza. Ramos won 37 of his 49 bouts, 23 by knockout. He was a crowd-pleaser. Everybody loved him and he loved everybody back, especially the women." (Photograph by Paul M. Orduna.)

Five

THE 1970S
"KING" CARLOS RULES
WITH A LEFT HOOK

So there was a hotshot named Nelson Ruiz, who was an up-and-coming sensation. I told (Palomino's manager) Jackie McCoy, "Let's find out about Carlos and fight this guy." Carlos was incredible (winning a six-round knockout). I remember walking up to Jackie afterward and saying "A Star is Born."

— Don Chargin, matchmaker at the Olympic Auditorium, as told to ESPN Boxing

The *Ring* magazine called the first "King" Carlos Palomino–Armando "The Man" Muniz battle one of the best fights of 1977. It was the first time in boxing history that two college graduates fought for the world title. Palomino received his bachelor's degree in recreation administration from Long Beach State, and Muniz graduated with a bachelor's degree in Spanish from Cal State Los Angeles. These crosstown rivals had many other similarities: both were born in Mexico, both came from large families, both were raised in Southern California, and both fought for the US Army.

In Palomino's first defense of his WBC welterweight title at the Olympic Auditorium, Muniz dropped him in the first round. Going into the 15th and final round, the fight was dead even. Palomino told the *Los Angeles Times*, "I went out and just threw everything I had for 2 1/2 minutes. Finally he went down." Though Muniz wept at the bouts conclusion, he said, "I am proud to say that Carlos and I were in that fight."

Carlos Palomino was a bit of a renaissance man: he was the first welterweight champion in the modern era to successfully defend his title four times in one year, appeared on the cover of the July 2, 1979, issue of *Sports Illustrated* battling it out with Roberto Duran, became an actor and a television pitchman for Miller Lite Beer ("But, Don't Drink the Water!"), and after retiring from boxing in 1979, perfected the art of the comeback (in 1997) by closing out his career with four victories in his last five fights at age 48.

Promoter Don Fraser told John Hall of the *Los Angeles Times* in 1971, "Boxing has never been healthier. But I know how we could make it even better . . . If we only had a Xerox machine that could run off 100 copies of Mando Muniz; if every arena had a Muniz, we'd all be in heaven."

In the early 1970s, brothers Ernie "Indian Red" Lopez (right) and Danny "Little Red" Lopez (left) were under the wing of the "Old Professor of Main St.," Howie Steindler (second from right). Bennie Georgino (second from left) took over management after the murder of Steindler. Danny expressed to *Boxing Today*, "He (Steindler) was like a father to me and as fine a man as I've met . . . every fight is a tribute to Howie."

California-born Don Fraser served as publicist at Hollywood Legion Stadium (1956–1959), Olympic Auditorium (1959–1967), and the Forum (1967–1981). Fraser's big break came in 1972 when Jack Kent Cooke appointed him as director of boxing at the Forum. Other jobs Fraser held in boxing were as a writer, matchmaker, and executive. Fraser (center) is shown in the early 1970s with retired boxers Enrique Bolanos (left) and Art Aragon (right) at the Spaghetti Factory in Hollywood.

Ruben Navarro, "The Maravilla Kid," defeated fellow Mexican American boxer Raul Rojas by a 10-round unanimous decision at the Olympic Auditorium on July 9, 1970. Navarro later recounted to the *Los Angeles Herald Examiner*, "One night we were all drinking it up at Mando Ramos house in Long Beach. It was a couple of days after I had beaten Raul Rojas at the Olympic. Raul kept telling me how he thought he had whipped me and that we should go outside and settle it once and for all. Well, after a few too many drinks, we finally went outside. We walked down to the beach and had it out. And I whipped Raul again." Navarro, a master at slipping punches, raises his arms in victory at the Olympic Auditorium while manager/trainer Johnny Flores (right) directs him. In the late 1940s, Flores started his own backyard gym in Pacoima, thus beginning a long career in boxing. Flores, nicknamed "Mr. Golden Gloves" and "Mr. Amateur Boxing," was a Purple Heart–decorated World War II veteran. (Photograph by Theo Ehret.)

Jimmy Lennon (right), ring announcer for the Olympic Auditorium from 1943 to 1986, stands with Luis Magana, who ran Olympic public relations for the Mexican press. Always attired in a tuxedo and possessing a rich tenor voice, the dapper Lennon called himself "The Irishman with a Mexican Accent." John Hall of the *Los Angeles Times* wrote that Lennon's "reputation as boxing's 'most dramatic MC' came mostly from his flowing Spanish introductions of Mexican fighters." Lennon told Hall he learned Spanish "all because of Maria Aguirre, my Spanish teacher at Venice High. I never had any other lessons." Lennon (a favorite of Mexican fight fans because of his perfect pronunciation) said to the *Ring*, "A man is entitled to the dignity of his own name." John Beyrooty, boxing beat writer for the *Los Angeles Herald Examiner*, said, "When you think about it, Jimmy did more for Mexican American relations in Los Angeles than anyone else." (Photograph by Vitico's Fotos.)

Los Angeles boxing aficionados mingle in the foyer of the Olympic Auditorium the evening Mando Ramos and Ultiminio "Sugar" Ramos waged their epic battle of August 6, 1970. An unforgettable aroma of beer, hot dogs, and sweat saturated the air in anticipation of an exciting night of fisticuffs. Note the painting (right) of revered Olympic Auditorium fighter Enrique Bolanos. (Photograph by George Rodriguez.)

The dawn of the 1970s found Mando Ramos reeling off the most impressive win trilogy in his career—beating former featherweight champions Ultiminio "Sugar" Ramos, Raul Rojas, and lightweight contender Ruben Navarro all in a row. The dressing room mood turns serious as Mando mentally prepares before his fight with "Sugar" at the Olympic Auditorium. Pictured, from left to right, are Mando, Bennie Georgino, Andy "Kid" Heilman, and comanagers Lee Prlia and Jackie McCoy. (Photograph by George Rodriguez.)

Above, in possibly his toughest battle ever, Mando Ramos (right) defeated Ultiminio "Sugar" Ramos in a tight, brutal 10-round split decision on August 6, 1970, in front of 10,400 screaming fans at the Olympic Auditorium. Matchmaker Don Chargin said, "The best fight I ever saw at the Olympic was Ramos vs. Ramos, without a doubt." The duel turned into a seesaw brawl, with enough leaning, damaging punches, and blood gushing to last a lifetime. The photograph below shows Chicano hometown hero Mando slowly walking to his corner, while the more experienced "Sugar" is on wobbly legs awaiting manager Pancho Rosales. Rick Farris remembers, "In the end it was Mando's fight, but he left the ring with major cuts over both eyes." Their congratulatory embrace after the bout flowed with mutual respect for one another. (Above, courtesy of Rudy Tellez; below, photograph by George Rodriguez.)

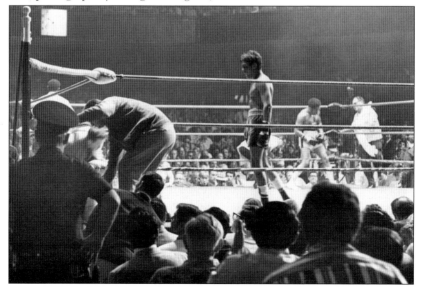

Long, lanky Mando Ramos was a two-time lightweight champion of the world who fought from 1965 to 1975, ending his career with 37 wins (23 knockouts), 11 losses, and 1 draw. Ramos is captured in all his damaged glory right after his fight with Cuban refugee Ultiminio "Sugar" Ramos, who fought out of Mexico City. This image was taken by Theo Ehret, house photographer of the Olympic Auditorium, who documented boxing history using a Rolleiflex camera.

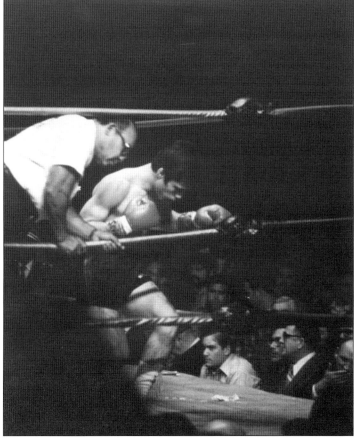

The uncrowned champion Armando "The Man" Muniz says a prayer in his corner as trainer Louie Jauregui (left) prepares to exit the ring. Announcer Jimmy Lennon of the Olympic Auditorium originally coined "The Man," saying Muniz was a "prime example of what a respectful and honest man should be." Muniz, of Montebello, fought from 1970 to 1978, leaving boxing with 44 wins (30 knockouts), 14 losses, and 1 draw. (Courtesy of Armando Muniz.)

MANDO

RAMOS

**Former World
Lightweight Champion**

OLYMPIC
AUDITORIUM
Thur. Nite 3
DEC.

LIGHTWEIGHTS - 10 RDS - NO TV

TICKET PRICES:
RINGSIDE $10.00
LOWER BALCONY $10.00
UPPER BALCONY $7.50
RESERVATIONS: RI 9-5171

Ex-Stablemates Collide

RAUL

ROJAS

**Former World
Featherweight Champio**

PROMOTER: AILEEN EATON   **MATCHMAKER: DON CHAR**

42 COLET POSTER PRINTING CO., 1333 W. 13th Place, L.A. 90015

Manager Jackie McCoy spoke of the upcoming December 10, 1970, grudge fight between former stablemates Mando Ramos and Raul Rojas at the Olympic Auditorium: "There is hate involved in this fight and I mean real hate. These guys aren't angels in or out of the ring." Rojas said, "I'll get those tender eyes of his open anyway I can and I do mean anyway. I used to destroy him when we sparred in front of a few fans in the gym for nothing. Now I get to do it in front of 10,000 people and get paid for it." Ramos countered, "I know that Raul is going to try and butt me and open my eyes. I want my lightweight championship back and this sawed-off loudmouth isn't going to stand in my way. I'm going to humiliate him in front of all his friends. He'll be sorry he ever agreed to the fight. When I get through with him, he'll be selling programs at my future fights." Former boxer and historian Rick Farris remembered, "A bitterness had developed many years earlier. When Mando was young, Rojas would pound his stablemate brutally. As Mando grew in size and ability, their gym wars would equal bouts of a championship level. Rojas still had one big payday looming and that would be with his former stablemate Ramos. A few weeks before the match, Mando and Stella Ramos's little boy, Armando Jr. celebrated his first birthday." An uninvited Rojas suddenly appears at the party and asks to speak to Mando in private. Farris continues, "Mando said Raul got very emotional, told him he was just talking big in the papers to pump up the box office. Rojas said he had not trained a day for the fight and planned on laying down after a few rounds. He asked Mando if he would 'take it easy' on him. Mando partied hard for more than a week. He missed days at the gym. One day he wanders into the gym and Jackie McCoy was livid. 'What in the hell are you doing? Rojas is working his ass off, reports say Raul is in the best shape in years!' It suddenly occurred to Mando he'd been had." Ramos KO'd Rojas in six.

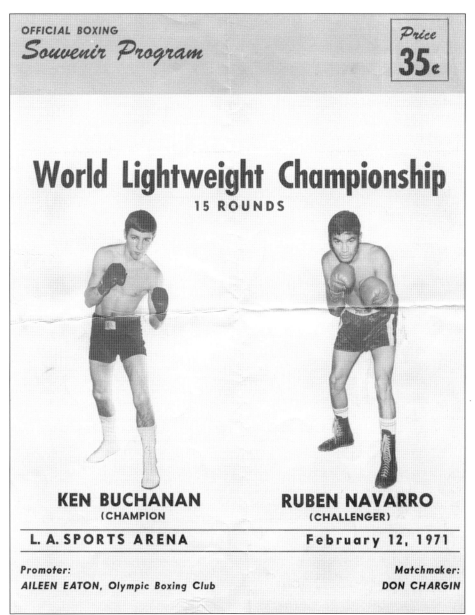

World Lightweight Championship
15 ROUNDS

KEN BUCHANAN
(CHAMPION

RUBEN NAVARRO
(CHALLENGER)

L. A. SPORTS ARENA   **February 12, 1971**

Promoter:
AILEEN EATON, Olympic Boxing Club

Matchmaker:
DON CHARGIN

Previously, Ruben Navarro had challenged Rene Barrientos, of the Philippines, for the vacant WBC super featherweight title on February 15, 1969, in Manila, but lost by a 15-round unanimous decision. When challenger Mando Ramos pulled out of his title shot against lightweight champion Ken Buchanan of Scotland due to a groin injury, No. 3 contender "The Maravilla Kid" Ruben Navarro got the nod to fight for the title. Navarro had been in training camp the past two weeks preparing for an upcoming scheduled bout with Jimmy Robertson and was in good condition. Navarro put up a strong effort, but lost a 15-round unanimous decision to Buchanan before 10,360 spectators at the Los Angeles Sports Arena on February 12, 1971. Navarro told the *Los Angeles Herald Examiner*, "I fought Buchanan on just 48 hours notice at the Sports Arena and I thought I beat him. But Buchanan's people brought in their own judge and ref and he got the decision. That's the way it goes."

This long-awaited neighborhood grudge match (Harbor vs. Maravilla) between former champion Mando Ramos (left) and Ruben Navarro would be for Los Angeles bragging rights of who was the best lightweight in town. Navarro said about their simmering feud, "I wouldn't say we are exactly friends, but we respect each other. One thing that really bugs me is the fact that Mando has had all the breaks *handed* to him so far, while I've had to *fight* for mine." Ramos responded by scoffing, "Navarro is building his reputation by beating a bunch of hamburgers." In the fight, Navarro outsmarted Ramos, who suffered from ring rust due to a nine-month absence—until Navarro was cut around the right eye. Ramos still won a close 10-round unanimous decision over Navarro at the Olympic Auditorium on September 30, 1971. (Below, courtesy of Rudy Tellez.)

Rodolfo "El Gato" Gonzalez, from Guadalajara, Jalisco, Mexico, began boxing in his native country by winning his first 33 bouts by knockout. Not satisfied with the pay scale in Mexico, Rodolfo migrated to Long Beach in 1963, arriving at the Seaside Gym (near the old Pike) under Bill Fields. After 76 fights, the career of "El Gato" ("The Cat") turned around when he signed with new manager Jackie McCoy in August 1971. The next year brought a key victory for "El Gato" when he belted out a 10-round majority decision victory over "The Maravilla Kid" Ruben Navarro at the Anaheim Convention Center on July 31, 1972. In only a little over a year under the wing of manager Jackie McCoy, Gonzalez lifted the WBC lightweight championship from Chango Carmona, of Mexico City, by a 12th-round TKO on November 10, 1972, at the Los Angeles Sports Arena. Gonzalez, a 3-1 underdog, gave Carmona such a beating that he was unable to answer the bell for the 13th round. Pictured celebrating the new championship are, from left to right, Jesse Reid (trainer), Cannonball Green (second), Gonzalez, and Jackie McCoy.

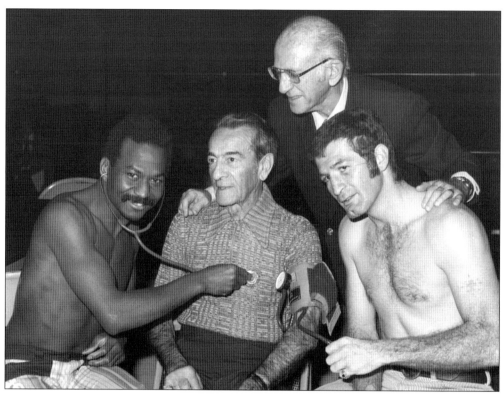

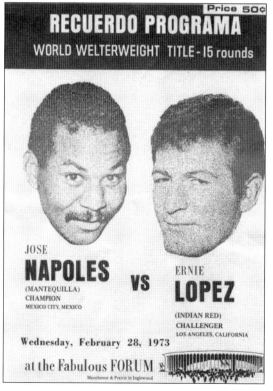

Price 50¢

RECUERDO PROGRAMA

WORLD WELTERWEIGHT TITLE - 15 rounds

JOSE
NAPOLES
(MANTEQUILLA)
CHAMPION
MEXICO CITY, MEXICO

VS

ERNIE
LOPEZ

(INDIAN RED)
CHALLENGER
LOS ANGELES, CALIFORNIA

Wednesday, February 28, 1973

at the Fabulous FORUM

Manchester & Prairie in Inglewood

Ernie "Indian Red" Lopez fought twice for the world welterweight title in front of sold-out crowds at the Forum, losing both times to WBC/WBA champion Jose "Mantequilla" ("Butter") Napoles, an expatriate Cuban fighting out of Mexico City. Boxing writer Dan Hafner wrote, "It is the misfortune of Ernie 'Indian Red' Lopez to come along when one of the all-time greats Jose Napoles rules the welterweight division." Pictured above, Napoles (left) brings some comic relief to the prefight medical examination as he checks out the heartbeat of Lopez's manager Howie Steindler while Dr. Jack Useem and Lopez (right) observe. In their first fight, Napoles won by TKO in the 15th round on February 14, 1970; and in their second matchup (program on the left), Napoles knocked Lopez out cold in the seventh round on February 28, 1973. As Lopez lay unconscious on the mat for three minutes, Napoles pleaded, "Please wake up!" Steindler said, "I never saw power like that."

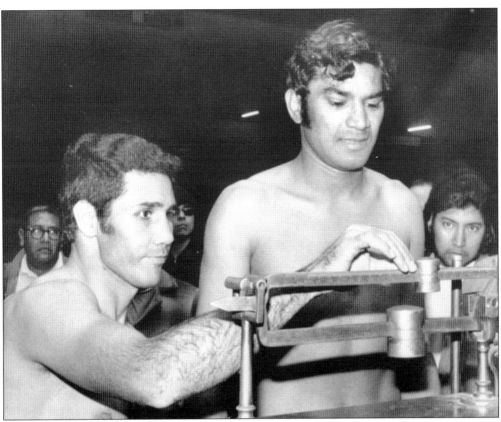

Rodolfo Gonzalez successfully defended his title twice during his WBC lightweight championship run from 1972 to 1974. Pictured above is the weigh-in for Gonzalez's first defense against Ruben Navarro (on scale). Gonzalez recalled to Dan Hanley, "Ruben (Navarro) was telling the press that after he knocked me out, he was going to throw me in a trashcan in the alley. It didn't turn out quite that way. I stopped him in nine." Navarro said, "This is not the same man I fought in Anaheim." Shown below, second Cannonball Green (left) is all smiles while ring announcer Jimmy Lennon raises Gonzalez's hand after he retained his lightweight title against Navarro at the Los Angeles Sports Arena on March 17, 1973. Gonzalez, a soft-spoken, religious man with a killer left hook to the liver, ended his career with a stellar record of 80 wins (67 knockouts), 8 losses, and 1 draw while fighting from 1959 to 1974.

Rising contender "Schoolboy" Bobby Chacon (left) meets up with rival Ruben "El Puas" Olivares, the hard-hitting former two-time bantamweight champion, in the makeshift gymnasium at the Alexandria Hotel in downtown Los Angeles in 1973, before the first of their three fights. (Photograph by Theo Ehret, courtesy of Brad Little.)

Olivares (right), the gold-toothed Mexico City playboy, handed Chacon the first loss of his career via a ninth-round TKO at the Forum on June 23, 1973. "Mr. Knockout" Olivares won the vacant NABF featherweight title when Chacon's manager, Joe Ponce, stopped the fight as Chacon could no longer continue. Chacon fondly spoke to *Sports Illustrated* about his two-acre ranch at the north end of the valley, "Olivares bought this place for me, and Danny Lopez furnished it."

The promotional boxing poster called it the "Blood and Guts Battle" between two of the finest top-ranked welterweight fighters that Los Angeles had to offer. At right, Armando "The Man" Muniz, originally from Delicias, Chihuahua, Mexico, throws a hard right to the cheek of the favored Ernie "Indian Red" Lopez. Below, referee John Thomas (left) pulls Muniz (center) away after an explosive combination floored Lopez in the seventh round of their bout at the Olympic Auditorium on July 26, 1973. Moments later, Lopez's manager, Howie Steindler, stopped the fight in between rounds, resulting in a TKO victory for Muniz. John Hall of the *Los Angeles Times* wrote about Muniz: "Inside the ring, he comes to make war, not love. He's never been in a dull fight. He's a roaring tiger willing to take two or three punches to land one." (Both, courtesy of Armando Muniz.)

"King" Carlos Palomino picked his opponents apart like a surgeon and had a dangerous reputation for throwing powerful left hooks to the body. Palomino fought from 1972 until his retirement in 1998, ending with a record of 31 victories (19 knockouts), 4 defeats, and 3 draws. Palomino, who was managed by Jackie McCoy and trained by Noe Cruz, is shown working out on the double-end bag at the Westminster Boxing Club in 1974. (Photograph by Theo Ehret.)

Frankie "Huero" ("Light-Skinned") Duarte was an all-action, relentless fighter from the rough part of Venice. Duarte finished boxing with a record of 47 wins (34 knockouts), 8 losses, and 1 draw during a career that lasted from 1973 to 1989. Along the way, Duarte won the California featherweight title in 1979 and the NABF bantamweight title in 1986. Duarte is shown hitting the heavy bag at the Teamsters Gym in 1974.

In one of the most exciting dream matches in Los Angeles boxing history, "Schoolboy" Bobby Chacon (23-1) of Sylmar knocked out Danny "Little Red" Lopez (23-0) of Alhambra in the ninth round to win the mythical "City Championship." This clash of local rising stars in the featherweight division occurred in front of a sold-out crowd of 16,027 at the Los Angeles Sports Arena on May 24, 1974. The fight produced so much interest that another 3,000 fans watched it on closed-circuit TV at the Olympic Auditorium. Chacon (left) was in his wheelhouse all night long, rocking Lopez repeatedly with his right hand throughout the fight. The *Los Angeles Times* reported, "In the ninth round [Joe] Ponce [Chacon's manager] ordered Chacon to finish off Lopez. 'I thought his [Lopez's] legs were giving out. I told Bobby to go get him.'" Chacon remembered, "That was my favorite time in boxing. I went on Johnny Carson and everything." (Below, courtesy of Rudy Tellez.)

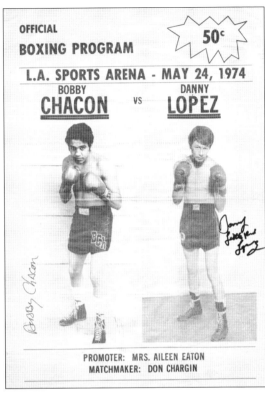

OFFICIAL
BOXING PROGRAM
50¢

L.A. SPORTS ARENA - MAY 24, 1974
BOBBY | DANNY
CHACON vs LOPEZ

PROMOTER: MRS. AILEEN EATON
MATCHMAKER: DON CHARGIN

In 1956, an eight-year-old Ersi Arvizu, along with sister Rosella and brother Art Jr., began singing Mexican ranchera songs during intermissions at the Olympic Auditorium on nights when their father and boxing manager, Art Arvizu, worked the corner of his fighters. In 1964, a family vocal group evolved named The Sisters (Mary, Rosella, and Ersi), who released three singles on the Del-Fi label. Ersi later sang the East L.A. anthem "Sabor A Mi" with the group El Chicano in 1971. Ersi quietly got into boxing in 1976, notching 1 win (with 1 knockout) and 1 loss as a professional, both at Hyatt Tahoe, Incline Village, Nevada. When a surprised Art saw his daughter's picture in a boxing magazine at a barbershop, he quickly informed his wife, Rita. Ersi left a promising career as a featherweight when her mother, embarrassed by the discovery, asked "Why are you boxing? This is a man's sport." Ersi, from the East Los Angeles barrio El Hoyo, is shown training at Hoover Street Gym in South Central Los Angeles in 1976. (Courtesy of Ersi Arvizu.)

"Schoolboy" Bobby Chacon drops Alfredo Marcano of Venezuela on his seat to capture the vacant WBC featherweight title by a ninth-round TKO at the Olympic Auditorium on September 7, 1974. On his way to the championship, Bobby had victories over "Tury" Pineda, Chucho Castillo, and Danny "Little Red" Lopez. West Coast matchmaker Don Chargin recalled Chacon as "a beautiful boxer who could bang. He had a ton of natural talent."

Jaime de Haro of Pronesa Promotions sits between WBC/WBA welterweight champion Jose "Mantequilla" Napoles (seated, second from left), and former NABF welterweight champion Armando Muniz as they shake hands at their March 1975 press conference at the Hotel Princesa in Acapulco, Guerrero, Mexico. Regarding the elusive title belt, Muniz's mother, Josefa, said, "Mijo [son] don't you understand? Maybe God has something else planned for you. Maybe it just wasn't meant to be." (Courtesy of Armando Muniz.)

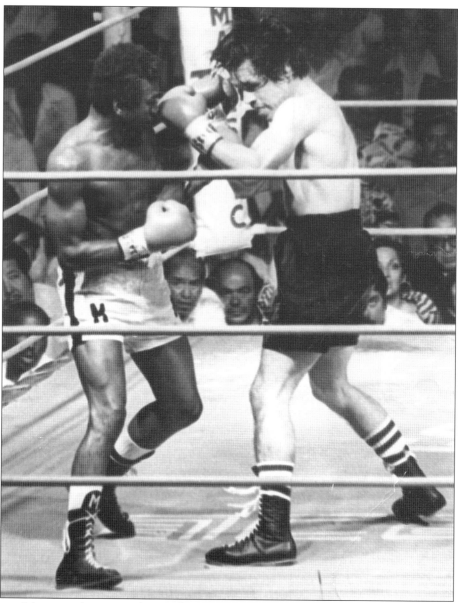

In one of the worst decisions in boxing history, challenger Armando Muniz (right) was robbed of the welterweight world championship on March 29, 1975, in his fight against Jose "Mantequilla" Napoles at the Convention Center in Acapulco. Muniz completely battered Napoles from pillar to post, turning his face into a bloody mess around his eyes, nose, and mouth. The drama unfolded when the fight was halted in the 12th round as Napoles was unable to continue due to cuts. Shockingly, the bout was awarded to Napoles on a technical decision and Muniz came home empty without the title. John Hall of the *Los Angeles Times* wrote, "Muniz had four shots at the welterweight crown. He won it at least once, pounding Jose Napoles to a pulp in Mexico. But they stole it, saying it was his head, not his fists that had slashed Napoles into spaghetti and meat balls. The president of Mexico gave Muniz a gold watch, but he wanted the belt." Muniz remembered, "To this day, I know I beat him, and [WBC commissioner] Jose Sulaiman knows that too." (Courtesy of Armando Muniz.)

CELEBREN
EL CINCO DE MAYO
en **DISNEYLANDIA**

Viva Mexico

Mayo 3 y 4

Abundancia de estrellas

LALO GONZALEZ "EL PIPORRO"
LUIS MANUEL PELAYO
DAVID REYNOSO
QUETA JIMENEZ
Gran Mariscal **BOBBY CHACON**
Campeón Mundial de Peso Pluma

TABASCO • LOS CAMPEROS
LEOPOLDO GONZALEZ • ANTONIO BRAVO • LOS GALLOS
ISELA SOTELO • MARIMBA MAYALANDIA
LOS ACAPULCO 4 • LOS CHANGUITOS FEOS DE TUCSON
MAESTRO DE CEREMONIAS **ANTONIO DE MARCO**

y grandioso desfile de 'VIVA MEXICO' con Mariachi
y Marimba! Además, 50 Atracciones y Aventuras!

Todo a precios populares!

Disneylandia

Abierto: **Sábado** Mayo 3 **Domingo**, Mayo 4 desde
desde las 8 a.m. hasta 7 p.m. las 8 a.m. hasta 9 p.m.

1ro. de Mayo de 1975, La Prensa de Los Angeles - Pag. 7

The flashy Bobby Chacon was the biggest "little" fighter in Los Angeles after knocking out Danny Lopez in a nontitle fight in 1974 and stopping Alfredo Marcano for the featherweight title a few months later. At a Cinco de Mayo Disneyland weekend celebration in 1975 (including various actors and singers from Mexico), the grand marshal of the Viva Mexico parade was Bobby Chacon, the featherweight champion of the world. After he lost his title to "Rockabye" Ruben Olivares on June 20, 1975, the joy of boxing began to fade for Chacon. John Hall of the *Los Angeles Times* wrote, "Chacon has already been there—World Featherweight Champ. Weight and musical chairs with managers and trainers got him. But he had two years in 1974 and 1975 like few ever. Now, at 27, he's in the midst of the longest on-and-off comeback in memory—maybe just a punch away from setting all the bells to ringing once again. And maybe not." A few years later in 1982, Chacon astonishingly turned the boxing world around by winning the title once again.

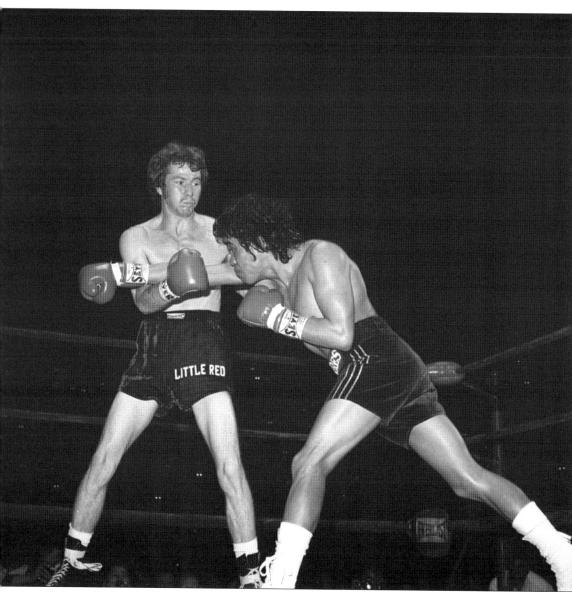

Exciting featherweight prospect Danny "Little Red" Lopez was climbing up the rankings when he met former two-time bantamweight and two-time featherweight champion of the world Ruben "El Puas" Olivares on December 4, 1975, at the Forum. Mexican boxing icon Olivares was considered one of the hardest-hitting bantamweight champions of all time while holding attendance records at the Fabulous Forum. An action-packed opening stanza saw Lopez get dropped by his idol Olivares, but Lopez wasted no time in proceeding to down Olivares twice in that same round. Lopez (left) delivered the final knockout blow in the seventh round to a still tough (but fading) Olivares. Lopez told *Boxing Illustrated*, "Ruben was my hero . . . beating him has to make a fellow feel like he had defeated Muhammad Ali. Olivares had to be one of my toughest. I felt every punch Olivares threw at me. But I am sure Ruben wasn't what he once was. I have to admit I didn't beat Olivares at his peak." (Photograph by Theo Ehret, courtesy of Brad Little.)

Bobby Chacon

"Schoolboy" Bobby Chacon was a slick, charismatic boxer out of San Fernando, California, who went all the way to become a two-time world champion. His road to boxing stardom was against all odds as his teenage résumé consisted of being a runaway, tough street fighter, and gang member. Chacon's wife, Valorie (Ginn), at first encouraged him to turn professional, telling *Sports Illustrated*, "I'd never seen him actually fight, but people would come to me after a street fight and say, 'You ought to have seen him.' So I told him he ought to try boxing." Chacon was one of the most exciting boxers of his era (1972–1988), as out of his 59 wins, 47 came by way of knockout—along with 7 losses and 1 draw. Manager Joe Ponce told *Sports Illustrated*, "God gave Bobby a heavy hand." Years later, Chacon recalled the dangers of being at the top to the *Los Angeles Times*: "After I became champion [in 1982], everything became a little haywire. I could have anything I wanted now, so I did."

Arturo Frias was a buzz saw style of fighter who was born and raised in the barrios of East Los Angeles. Frias left Roosevelt High School to get into boxing and shot out of the gate winning his first 20 fights with his gutsy, brawling style. Frias (center) is shown in 1976 with comanager/trainer Al Lira (left) and comanager/Los Angeles–based attorney Norman Kaplan (right). (Courtesy of Arturo Frias.)

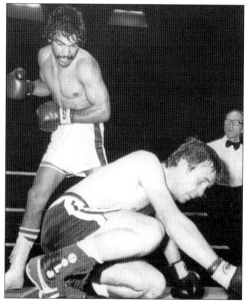

The first fight outside of Southern California for Carlos Palomino was all the way in Empire Pool (Wembley Arena) in London, England, where challenger Palomino hammered away the WBC welterweight championship belt from John H. Stracey with a 12-round TKO on June 22, 1976. Referee Sid Nathan (right) looks on as Palomino's (left) arsenal of uppercuts and stinging left hooks to the liver dropped Stracey (center) twice to end the fight. Palomino, a 10-1 underdog, shocked Stracey's promoter, Mickey Duff, and manager so much with his performance that *Sports Illustrated* reported both "rushed off to take another look at tapes of previous Palomino fights. They figured McCoy (Palomino's manager) had slipped in a ringer." (Courtesy of Carlos Palomino.)

Promoter Aileen Eaton's focus at the Olympic Auditorium was aimed at the Mexican American population of Los Angeles, whereas rival promoter George Parnassus's fight cards at the Forum attracted more the Mexican nationals. Eaton, who was called "Mrs. Boxing" by noted *Los Angeles Times* columnist Jim Murray, said, "I think local Mexican Americans make up about 60 percent of our audience." Eaton, shown at the Olympic in June 1976, installed a star-making machinery in the development and promotion of her young fighters' careers. "We operate under the theory, too, that we must develop young fighters," Eaton said. "Without that there is no boxing." She created maximum newspaper buzz around her family of boxers. Eaton's formula for grooming her boxers turned them into local attractions during her weekly televised boxing shows, building them up until they hit future big paydays as champions.

JESUS PIMENTEL
1er. GALLO del MUNDO Manager Harry Kabakoff

NABF bantamweight titlist Jesus "Chucho" Pimentel was born in Sayula, Jalisco, Mexico, but grew up in the San Gabriel Valley and East Los Angeles. In a career that lasted from 1960 to 1971, "Little Poison" was one of the greatest knockout artists in bantamweight history and possibly the best bantamweight to never win a world title. Pimentel had an outstanding record of 77 wins (69 knockouts) and 7 losses, but did not challenge for the title until his last fight in 1971. Perhaps it was an indifferent promoter, George Parnassus, or an overprotective manager, Harry Kabakoff, that cost Pimentel a chance at the title in his prime. John Hall of the *Los Angeles Times* wrote, "Pimentel was the prettiest little bantamweight around—a 118-pound assassin with 300-pound fists. He could knock your head off with a left hook and once rolled up something like 30 straight knockouts. He didn't get his title fight at the right time. His best was already used up when he met Ruben Olivares. But he was No. 1 for a long time and he had the moments."

Originally from Palo Verde in Chavez Ravine, Rudy Tellez (right) stands next to his mentor Howie Steindler at the Main St. Gym in 1976. After Steindler's untimely death in 1977, Tellez helped run the Main St. Gym along with Carol Steindler and Johnny "The Flash" Ortiz until 1984. At one time the youngest manager in boxing, Tellez guided Joey Olivo to the WBA light flyweight championship in 1985. (Courtesy of Rudy Tellez.)

Trainer Noe Cruz (left) assists WBC welterweight champion Carlos Palomino with his gloves during a 1977 public workout at Sigler Park in Westminster. Palomino was training for his first title defense against Armando Muniz, who he later described as having "the best chin" he ever faced. Born in San Luis B. Sanchez ("El 57"), Sonora, Mexico, Palomino arrived to the United States at age 10 to become Orange County's own homegrown world champion. (Courtesy of Carlos Palomino.)

Defending WBC welterweight champion Carlos Palomino (left) trades shots with challenger Armando Muniz in their title fight at the Olympic Auditorium on January 21, 1977. Palomino dropped Muniz with a left hook in the 15th round, giving him a TKO victory when referee John Thomas stopped the fight with only 36 seconds left to go. Many boxing scholars called it the "Fight of the Year," and it was the first time in boxing history that two college graduates fought for a world title. Palomino told Dan Hanley of the Cyber Boxing Zone website, "I knew he [Armando] would stay on your chest. Sure enough, he started fast, decked me in the first round and controlled the first half of the fight. Then I started coming on in the second half. Jackie [McCoy] told me before the start of the 15th round that this was a toss-up. And sure enough the fight was dead even on the officials card. The winner of the last round would win the fight and I managed to stop Mando in the last round. It was a war." (Courtesy of Armando Muniz.)

Above, the two top bantamweights of Los Angeles—Alberto "Tweety" Davila (left) and Frankie "Huero" Duarte—were on a collision course to meet June 9, 1977, at the Olympic Auditorium in a WBC-sanctioned elimination bout billed as "D Day." Duarte told Dan Hanley of the Cyber Boxing Zone website, "I was in need of a real trainer at that point. I was not ready and was a mess. I wasn't training. I had nothing. Davila hit me with a little left hook in the third and I go down. I was stopped in five." Duarte was overweight, drinking, and smoking PCP up until two weeks before the fight. Davila, who later said, "I couldn't miss that night," is shown buckling Duarte's (left) knees with a textbook-style right hand in the image at right. (Both photographs by Theo Ehret.)

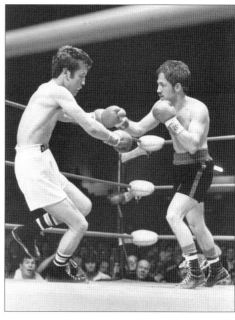

Since 1960, Howie Steindler was the no-nonsense proprietor of the Main St. Gym. Steindler, shown relaxing in his office in 1977, was the role model for the crusty trainer played in the *Rocky* movie. On November 6, 1976, Steindler achieved his dream of managing a world champion when Danny "Little Red" Lopez won the title. But on March 9, 1977, Steindler, 72, was murdered in a mob-style hit while driving home in his new gold Cadillac—a case that remains unsolved to this day.

MAIN EVENT - JULY 28, 1977
ALBERTO SANDOVAL vs. ALBERTO MORALES

Best wishes
Aileen Eaton

CARLOS PALOMINO
WELTERWEIGHT CHAMPION

DANNY LOPEZ
FEATHERWEIGHT CHAMPION

ALBERTO SANDOVAL
"SUPERFLY"

Souvenir of Aileen Eaton's 35th Anniversary of Boxing Promotion At The Olympic

Aileen Eaton, the most successful female promoter in boxing history, celebrates her 35th anniversary at the Olympic Auditorium on July 28, 1977. The former Aileen LeBell began as business manager for promoter Cal Eaton (whom she later married), working her first show at the Olympic on July 21, 1942. The fiery redhead Eaton was a marketing and creative genius in charge of the longest-running weekly boxing club in history until her retirement in 1980.

Joey Olivo, posing in the office of the Main St. Gym in 1979, was from the tough Ramona Gardens Housing Projects in Boyle Heights. Mexican fans nicknamed him "El Palo Que No Quiebra" ("The Stick That Doesn't Break"), but Olivo had two secret weapons over his opponents in the 108-pound division: his 5-foot, 8-inch height advantage and his 73-inch wingspan. Below, Olivo (a stick-and-move specialist) savors his 13th consecutive victory with a 10-round unanimous decision over Candy Iglesias on February 25, 1978, at the Forum as manager Rudy Tellez (left) joins in on the celebration. With so few American boxers in the flyweight division, Olivo had to travel to exotic locations such as South Korea, Chile, Panama, and Venezuela just to find work. Fighting from 1976 to 1989, Olivo ended his career with 39 wins (11 knockouts) and 8 losses. (Right, courtesy of Rudy Tellez; below, courtesy of Joey Olivo.)

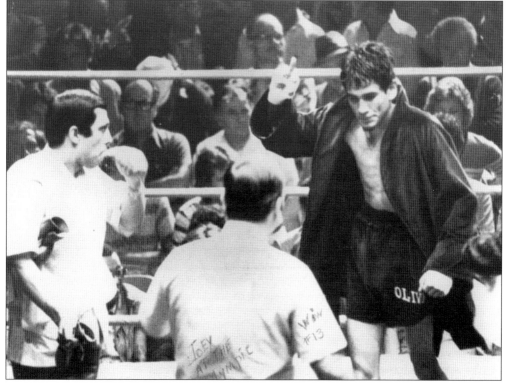

Mike Casey at Boxing.com described Danny "Little Red" Lopez as having "that tall and rangy frame and that eternal glint in his eye of the natural born hunter. The moustache that later accompanied the famous shock of bushy, red hair would perfectly complement the appearance of an old-style gunfighter out-of-time." Lopez (left) is shown at the entrance of the Main St. Gym in the late 1970s with his manager, Bennie Georgino.

In only his eighth fight, hard-hitting lightweight Herman "Kid" Montes of Pico Rivera remained undefeated by winning his first 10-round main event at the Olympic Auditorium with a unanimous decision over Jose Olivares on March 9, 1978. Up in the ring are, from left to right, Bob Castillo (sponsor), John Montes Sr. (father/ trainer), "Pops" Freddie Merino (assistant), Montes, Bennie Georgino (manager), John Thomas (referee) raising Montes's hand, and Jimmy Lennon (ring announcer).

The charismatic Alberto "Superfly" Sandoval, of Pomona, California, became the crowd favorite at the Olympic Auditorium, literally fighting his entire career there. Sandoval was a classy fighter who rose to be the No. 1–ranked bantamweight contender by the WBA. "Superfly" Sandoval, known for his quickness in the ring, ended with a career record of 32 wins (21 knockouts) and 5 losses while fighting from 1975 to 1982. Superfly (right) gets into the Easter spirit with opponent Eliseo Cosme of Mexico to promote their upcoming bantamweight face-off. The speedy Sandoval knocked out Cosme in five rounds at the Olympic Auditorium on March 23, 1978, avenging his first loss to Cosme a month earlier. Sandoval recalled, "When Jimmy Lennon asked about my nickname, I thought about 'Little Spanish Fly,' but went with 'Superfly' instead." Managed by Jackie McCoy and trained by Tony Cerda, Sandoval fought for the world title against WBC bantamweight champion Lupe Pintor of Mexico City but lost by a 12-round TKO at the Olympic Auditorium on February 9, 1980.

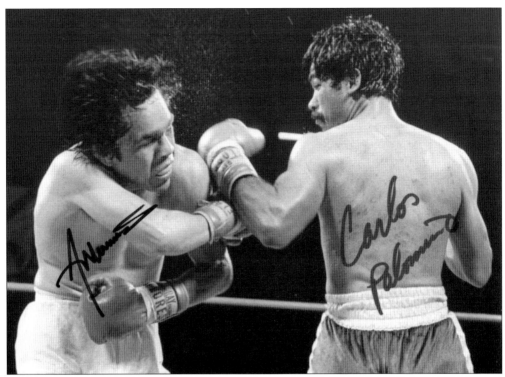

On May 27, 1978, Armando "The Man" Muniz would make his fourth and final attempt to capture a world title in the rematch bout with WBC welterweight champion Carlos Palomino at the Olympic Auditorium. Palomino, who held the crown from 1976 to 1979, was making his seventh title defense against the bruising puncher Muniz. But on this night, all of Muniz's tough ring wars from the 1970s would catch up with him. By the seventh round, Muniz realized that "something was terribly wrong . . . my reflexes were gone," as he was getting caught with punches he normally would have avoided. Above at right, Palomino throws a hard left at crosstown rival Muniz en route to a 15-round unanimous decision victory. Below, enjoying his celebrity status as champion, Palomino (left) shakes hands with comedian Don Rickles on *The Tonight Show* in 1978. (Above, courtesy of Armando Muniz; below, courtesy of Carlos Palomino.)

Oscar "The Boxer" Muniz, who attended Salesian High School in Boyle Heights, was a world-class bantamweight boxer who used his speed and power to full advantage to capture the NABF and USBA bantamweight titles. In a career that spanned from 1976 to 1986, Muniz, fighting out of Pico Rivera, ended with a record of 38 wins (22 knockouts), 7 losses, and 4 draws. Muniz (in robe), shown with manager Bennie Georgino at the Olympic Auditorium in 1978, left Georgino when he became frustrated while waiting around for a title shot.

The heavily tattooed Eddie "The Animal" Lopez was the heavyweight champ of the Eastside. Lopez, a tough street fighter from the Ramona Gardens Housing Projects in Boyle Heights, fought from 1976 to 1984, ending with 25 wins (17 knockouts), 4 losses, and 2 draws. Lopez (left) celebrates his 10-round decision victory over S.T. Gordon of Las Vegas at the Pico Rivera Sports Arena on August 28, 1978, with manager Ralph Gambina (center) and trainer/brother-in-law Al DeNava (right).

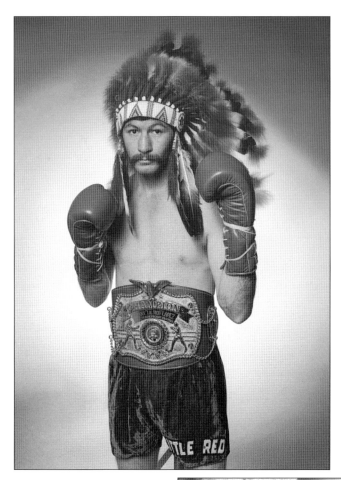

Of Ute Indian, Mexican, and Irish heritage, Danny "Little Red" Lopez was a notorious slow starter who became most dangerous after being knocked down. A fan favorite of the Olympic Auditorium, Lopez ended with 42 career victories (39 knockouts) and 6 losses while fighting from 1971 to 1992. Lopez, of Alhambra, notched eight successful defenses of his title while WBC featherweight champion from 1976 to 1980, and made the prestigious cover of *Sports Illustrated* on February 12, 1979, wearing his Native American headdress. (Photograph by Theo Ehret.)

Herman "Kid" Montes (center) is surrounded by his father/trainer, John Montes Sr. (left), and manager, Bennie Georgino, in the hallway of the Olympic Auditorium while warming up for his fight against German Cuello on May 24, 1979. Fighting from 1977 to 1985, Montes retired with an impressive career record of 32 wins (20 knockouts), 4 losses, and 4 draws, but, due to the politics of boxing, never got that elusive title shot. (Photograph by Mike Hollingsworth.)

Top-ranked featherweight Ruben Castillo, fighting out of Bakersfield, was a popular Los Angeles–area boxer. Castillo fought from 1975 to 1997, ending with 69 victories (37 knockouts), 10 losses, and 2 draws while picking up the USBA featherweight and WBO NABO lightweight titles along the way. Castillo had four unsuccessful tries at the world title. In a matter of unfortunate timing, he went up against three future Hall of Famers—Alexis Arguello, Salvador Sanchez, and Julio Cesar Chavez—and one dangerous Juan La Porte. Above, No. 1 contender (42-0) Ruben Castillo (seated) signs a contract in 1979 to fight featherweight champion Danny "Little Red" Lopez (left) while Castillo's manager Raul Garza (third from left), and promoter Harry Kabakoff (right) look on. The fight never happened as Lopez's management opted to fight Salvador Sanchez instead. Shown below celebrating in the catacombs of the Olympic Auditorium are, from left to right, James Castillo (brother/cornerman), Gene Aguilera, Castillo, and Tony Rivera (trainer).

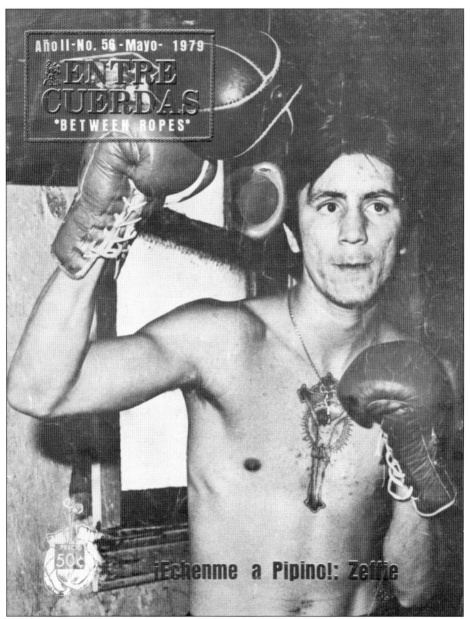

Año II- No. 56 -Mayo- 1979

ENTRE CUERDAS
"BETWEEN ROPES"

PRECIO 50¢

¡Echenme a Pipino!: Zeffie

Zeferino "Zeffie" Gonzalez, also called "Speedy," was a six-foot-tall, lanky welterweight boxer from Pico Rivera who fought from 1975 to 1983, finishing with a record of 21 wins (5 knockouts), 7 losses, and 1 draw. Zeffie's most memorable fight was against the legendary Roberto Duran (68-1), near the peak of his career, held at Caesars Palace in Las Vegas on September 28, 1979. Zeffie used his height, reach, and snappy jab to frustrate the charging Duran during the bout shown nationwide on ABC's *Wide World of Sports*. Even though Gonzalez lost a 10-round unanimous decision to Duran, he gave a good showing of himself on the big stage, with many in the audience claiming a draw. Sportscaster Howard Cosell commented afterwards, "Had Gonzalez had better punching power, it could have taken a different turn of events. But as I suggested at the outset of the bout, Gonzalez with that angular and suspiciously strong body . . . did put up a whale of a show." (Courtesy of Jose Vazquez De La Torre.)

Six

The 1980s
Thrills and Chills
with "Schoolboy"

Hurry home early, hurry on home
Boom Boom Mancini is fighting Bobby Chacon

—Warren Zevon, from "Boom Boom Mancini," on the album *Sentimental Hygiene*

Enduring a life of drama inside the ring and a life of tragedy outside the ring was a way of life for "Schoolboy" Bobby Chacon during the 1980s. Upset that Chacon would not quit boxing, his wife, Valorie, committed suicide in 1982. He became divorced from his second wife, spent time in jail in 1987 for violation of parole, and, four years later, his son Bobby "Chico" Chacon Jr. was the victim of a gang-related slaying.

His duels with Rafael "Bazooka" Limon (1982) and Cornelius Boza-Edwards (1983) were of legendary status (both were proclaimed as "Fight of the Year" by the *Ring* magazine). As one of the most thrilling boxers of his era, Chacon made his comeback complete by winning the super featherweight championship in the Limon battle.

After being stripped of his belt by the WBC, Chacon made one last try for the title in 1984. Jumping up in weight class to challenge Ray "Boom Boom" Mancini for the lightweight belt, Chacon's reflexes were just not there anymore. Chacon could not escape Mancini's damaging punches as he lay against the ropes absorbing punishment. The boxing wars and his no-defense style finally caught up with Chacon, and he retired for good in 1988.

Boxing was a natural progression for Joey Olivo, who had his fair share of street fights in East Los Angeles. Olivo tattooed his gang name "La Hazard Grande" ("Big Hazard") on his left forearm, but slowly began to break away from his barrio friends. After they began to see his name in the newspapers for boxing, they understood why.

Negotiations began in July 1984 for top contender Olivo to get a title shot. After eight long months of postponements, his purse was only to be $2,600. The bout finally took place in Miami, where Olivo was crowned the first American-born light flyweight champion of the world, a sacrifice and price Olivo never regretted. Not bad for a kid from the projects.

Eddie "The Animal" Lopez (right), in a hooded sweatshirt, and local boxing manager Ricardo Maldonado (left) are in reflective moods at the Main St. Gym. After Lopez lost a disputed decision to "Big" John Tate in 1977, he told the *Ring* magazine, "I seem to be doing better in the movies than in professional boxing. Maybe my future is really in Hollywood." Lopez was on a cinematic roll, appearing in three boxing movies—*Rocky II, The Champ*, and *The Main Event*. Lopez met former WBC/WBA heavyweight champion Leon Spinks at the Aladdin in Las Vegas on March 8, 1980, with the fight ending in a controversial 10-round draw. After Spinks butted Lopez earlier in the fight, The Animal reverted to his street-fighting mentality and butted him back in retaliation. For this, referee Mills Lane deducted a point from Lopez in the fifth round, costing him the victory. Lopez said, "More important than fighting for a title, was that I got to show the world that if you do me . . . I do you, only better." (Photograph by Carlos Baeza.)

Eddie "The Animal" Lopez (right) flashes the letter "H" in salute to his Big Hazard gang while in the ring with trainer Red Shannon in the image above. During a sparring session with an out-of-shape, 38-year-old Muhammad Ali at the Main St. Gym in 1980, Lopez taunted Ali by calling him "a fat old man" and challenged Ali by saying he would fight him for "two dollars." Using his street smarts, Lopez was hoping to lure Ali into a profitable fight. Rumors began to swirl of an HBO fight in Honolulu, Hawaii, where "The Greatest," Ali, would use this bout as a tune-up in quest of his fourth title against WBC heavyweight champion Larry Holmes. Alas, the Eastside's dream fight of Ali–Lopez never happened. Below, Lopez trains at the Olympic Gym in the early 1980s, with his protective cup reading "El Animal Chingon" ("The Animal the Baddest"). (Both photographs by Carlos Baeza.)

Fight manager Bennie Georgino celebrated his 60th birthday in 1980 at Little Joe's Italian American restaurant in the Chinatown district of Los Angeles. From left to right are (first row) Tommy Georgino, Sabu Chitjian, Bennie Georgino, Danny Lopez, and Bonnie Lopez; (second row) Mike Chitjian, Mario Portillo, Oscar Muniz, Memo Soto (trainer), unidentified, Jaime Garza, Herman Montes, unidentified, Johnny "Wito" Montes, Alberto Davila, and John Montes Sr.

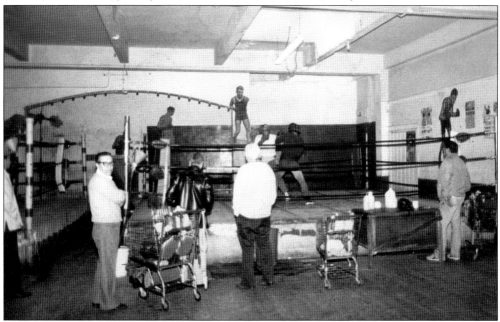

The Main St. Gym, seen here in the early 1980s, was located at 318 1/2 South Main Street in downtown Los Angeles, right on the edge of Skid Row. Since 1951, this location (the former Adolphus Theatre) was transformed into the center of all pugilistic activity in town and a hangout for the fight mob. Entrance into the school of hard knocks was under a painted sign that read "World Rated Boxers Train Here Daily."

The Arturo Frias story took a dreamlike, incredible turn when he fought WBA lightweight champion Claude Noel of Trinidad for the title on only 11 days notice. This Cinderella story was made possible when scheduled challenger Gonzalo Montellano injured his hip and had to bow out. A 5-1 underdog, Frias said that "Christmas came early" when he knocked out Noel with a right hand to the jaw in the eighth round to win the lightweight title at the Showboat Hotel & Casino in Las Vegas on December 5, 1981. History was made that evening as Frias became the first boxer in the modern era who was born and raised in East Los Angeles proper to win a world championship. Soon after, Frias defended his title against former champion Ernesto Espana of Venezuela by a ninth-round technical decision victory at the Olympic Auditorium on January 30, 1982. Frias, who later moved to Montebello, California, ended his career with 28 wins (8 knockouts) and 5 losses, while fighting from 1975 to 1985.

In this image, Frankie Baltazar (right), from the fighting Baltazar family of La Puente (with younger brothers Tony and Bobby), is about to knock out Abe Perez, of Tijuana, Baja California, Mexico, in the second round of their June 26, 1982, bout at the Olympic Auditorium. During his career, Frankie was comanaged and trained by his father, Frank "kiki" Baltazar Sr., along with assistant trainer John Martinez. Baltazar's most dramatic fight was against fellow southpaw Juan Escobar, also of Tijuana, who battered Baltazar's face swollen, closing both his eyes. Baltazar floored the rugged Escobar (who drew against the late, great Salvador Sanchez) with only 30 seconds to go, pulling out a tight 10-round split decision victory at the Olympic Auditorium on June 17, 1983. Disappointed over never getting a title shot, Baltazar explained to Dan Hanley what comanager Jackie McCoy had told him: "But when it was over, he took me aside and said to me that just being a fighter takes a very special person. And that made it easier to accept." (Photograph by Carlos Baeza.)

Above, Johnny "Wito" Montes (left) pounds Manuel Abedoy of Mexico against the ropes en route to a second-round knockout at the Olympic Auditorium on June 26, 1982, upping his record to 22-0 with 17 knockouts. Below, Montes (center) and manager Bennie Georgino (right) are interviewed by boxing television broadcaster Tom Kelly (left) after the Abedoy fight. In a career that lasted from 1979 to 1994, he faced such notable world champions as Pernell Whitaker, Hector "Macho" Camacho, Cornelius Boza-Edwards, and Hilmer Kenty in nontitle bouts. Montes ended his career with a sterling record of 43 wins (30 knockouts) and 6 losses, but, due to questionable managerial decisions, he was never able to secure a shot at the title. (Both photographs by Carlos Baeza.)

Popular lightweight boxer Johnny "Wito" Montes of Whittier exits the ring with his father/trainer, John Montes Sr., behind him after the Manuel Abedoy fight at the Olympic Auditorium in 1982. Montes, who attended El Rancho High School in Pico Rivera, was known for his devastating body punches while winning both the WBC Continental Americas light welterweight title and California light welterweight title in 1986. Montes's most memorable fight was vs. "Fearless" Freddie Pendleton, of Miami, Florida, at the Forum on November 22, 1988, when Montes came off the canvas in the second round to post a dramatic win. Montes recalled: "I come back to the corner in the later rounds . . . exhausted . . . telling my father [John Montes Sr.] 'I wish I had a cold beer' and my dad said, 'Well, get in there, son, and knock him out, and we'll get you all the beer you want!'" Montes was behind on all three scorecards when he knocked out Pendleton in the 10th and final round. (Photograph by Carlos Baeza.)

Tony "The Tiger" Baltazar of La Puente was known for his powerful left hook as he campaigned in the lightweight and junior welterweight divisions. Baltazar (nationally recognized for his prime time CBS Sports television appearances) had his biggest career victory with a 10-round unanimous decision over former WBA super featherweight champion Roger Mayweather "The Black Mamba" at the Country Club in Reseda on July 8, 1984. In the photograph above, Baltazar enters the ring with announcer Jimmy Lennon Jr. (standing left) for his bout against Raul Bencomo of Mexico, whom he knocked out in two rounds on June 26, 1982, at the Olympic Auditorium. In the image at right, Baltazar signals No. 1 alongside father/manager Frank "kiki" Baltazar Sr. (right). Unsuccessful in two attempts at the title vs. Hector "Macho" Camacho in 1990 and Carlos "Bolillo" Gonzalez, of Mexico City, in 1993, Baltazar retired with a record of 38 wins (30 knockouts), 7 losses, and 1 draw while fighting from 1979 to 2002. (Both photographs by Carlos Baeza.)

Alberto Sandoval was nicknamed "Superfly" for his flashy demeanor in and out of the ring. His strut, pompadour, and stylish clothes rightfully earned him the name. During an amateur exhibition at Chino State Prison in 1972, Sandoval entered the ring as a novice flyweight and recalled, "It was right at the time when *Superfly* was out by Curtis Mayfield and in the second round, an inmate yells out, 'Hey, Superfly!' and it stuck." In the image on the left, Sandoval (right) is shown in his fashionable long robe and with a lollipop in his mouth, with trainer Tony Cerda (center) nearby. Below, Sandoval (left) returns to the ring after a two-year absence to face Alberto Davila at the Olympic Auditorium in 1982. The artistic lens of photographer Carlos Baeza (using his Leica M4-P camera) captures both moments.

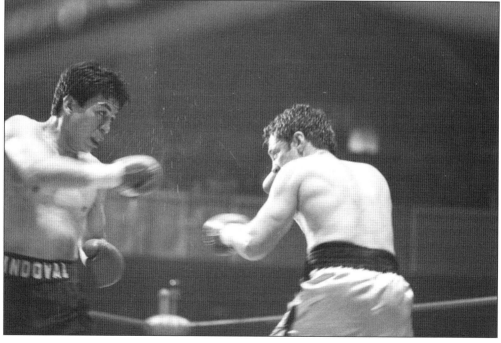

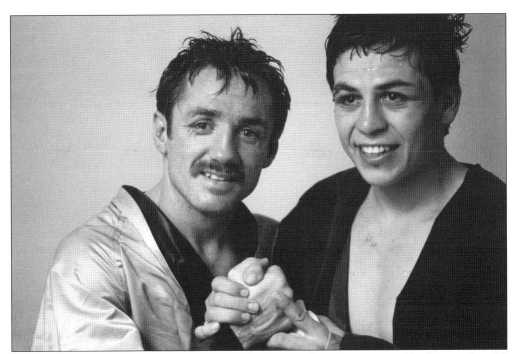

In a natural neighborhood rivalry matchup (both were from Pomona, and both were friends) sharpshooting Alberto "Tweety" Davila (left) defeated Alberto "Superfly" Sandoval by a 10-round decision at the Olympic Auditorium on November 18, 1982. Davila told Dan Hanley of the Cyber Boxing Zone website, "We knew each other for years, we even attended the same high school. Superfly had personality, good looks, and the crowd loved him." (Photograph by Carlos Baeza.)

Frankie Baltazar was a flashy left-hander from La Puente and a top world-ranked junior lightweight boxer who reeled off 28 wins in his first 30 fights. Known for his floppy mane, Baltazar compiled a distinguished lifetime ring record of 40 wins (26 knockouts), 3 losses, and 1 draw in a career that lasted from 1976 to 1991. In this image, Baltazar is shown at the Olympic Gym in 1982. (Photograph by Carlos Baeza.)

ENTRE CUERDAS

Precio c 50

BETWEEN ROPES

"SCHOOLBOY" BOBBY
CHACON

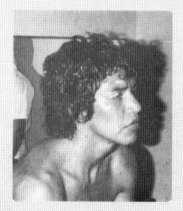

RAFAEL BAZOOKA
LIMON

ELIMINATION
Jr. Lightweights 130 LBS

Año-III-Núm. 76 - Mar. de 1980

Los Angeles. Call

Bobby Chacon fought like a man possessed in his monumental battle with WBC super featherweight champion Rafael "Bazooka" Limon of Mexico City on December 11, 1982. The following excerpts are from Mike Casey's essay "Helter Skelter: The Brutal Rock 'n' Roll Ride of Bobby Chacon" on East Side Boxing.com: "One of the great boxing rivalries was born. The two men plainly didn't like each other . . . If Chacon ever had a soul mate in courage and adversity, it was surely the brawling never-say-die Limon . . . When he hooked up with Bazooka for the fourth and final time at the Memorial Auditorium in Sacramento, Chacon dusted off an old canvas he had stored in the attic of his memory and set about painting his masterpiece . . . To this day, Chacon-Limon IV haunts my mind in the most wonderfully uplifting way . . . He [Chacon] surged down the final stretch, decking Limon in the 15th round to wrap up an epic triumph by unanimous decision." This bout marked Chacon's second and final championship belt in his illustrious career. (Courtesy of Jose Vazquez De La Torre.)

THE FORUM

The Forum (located at the corner of Manchester and Prairie in Inglewood) was built by Jack Kent Cooke in 1967 as a circular arena with scalloped edging at the top of its 80 Roman-inspired columns. The Forum staged its first boxing card (18,334 capacity) on June 14, 1968, made complete by cherry bomb explosions and a ring appearance by sex film actress Edy Williams. Jerry Buss purchased the Fabulous Forum in 1979 and held boxing shows from 1982 to October 1999.

Carol Steindler (center), daughter of Howie Steindler, stands with brothers "Kiko" Bejines (left) and Oscar "Negro" Bejines (right) of Guadalajara, Jalisco, Mexico, at the Main St. Gym in 1982. After Howie's death in 1977, Carol ran the Main St. Gym until it was demolished in 1984. When Jack Needleman, owner of the Olympic Auditorium, called to offer her space for a new Main St. Gym location, Carol moved the business to 1832 South Hope Street, Los Angeles, where it operated from 1984 to 1991.

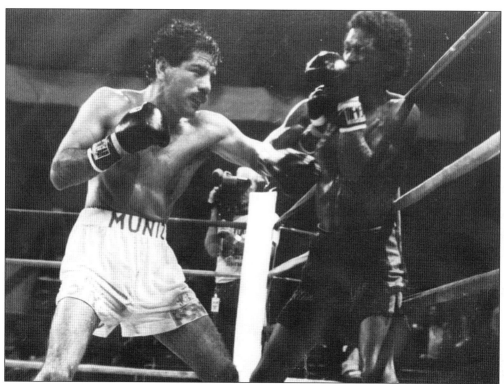

Above at left, Oscar "The Boxer" Muniz throws a hard left at WBA bantamweight champion "Joltin" Jeff Chandler (31-0) of Philadelphia en route to a nontitle, 10-round split decision victory at the Sands Casino Hotel in Atlantic City, New Jersey, on July 23, 1983. Below, Armando Muniz lifts up Oscar Muniz, who was a 10-1 underdog, in celebration of his career-defining victory, which was televised on ABC's *Wide World of Sports*. As Chandler (in background with robe) looks on in disbelief over the results, Muniz's manager/television director Howard Storm (right) rushes in. Oscar recalled, "It was a helluva fight. Nobody took a step back. Having my cousin Armando Muniz in my corner, there was no way I was going to let the family heritage down. At 122 pounds, I felt stronger. This was my weight at 27 years of age." (Both, courtesy of Oscar Muniz.)

Richie Sandoval of Pomona made his professional debut in 1980 and remained undefeated until a brutal knockout ended his career in 1986. Richie, the younger brother of bantamweight Alberto Sandoval, won the WBA bantamweight championship in a major upset by dethroning Jeff Chandler (making his tenth defense) via a 15-round TKO on April 7, 1984, at the Sands Casino Hotel in Atlantic City. Sandoval made two successful title defenses, but began having problems making the 118-pound limit. After taking four nontitle fights above the bantamweight limit, Sandoval made the strategic error of dropping back down in weight to fight again, as the WBA threatened to strip him of his title for failure to stage a title defense in almost 1 1/2 years. Extremely weakened by having to lose 10 pounds in the week leading up to his title fight against Gaby Canizales of Laredo, Texas, Sandoval followed a diet of not eating any solid foods—living only on minimal amounts of water. Sandoval was dropped four times during the fight before experiencing a frightening seventh-round TKO loss to Canizales at Caesars Palace, Las Vegas on March 10, 1986. Sandoval was knocked unconscious for 15 minutes and suffered life-threatening brain injuries, prompting promoter Bob Arum of Top Rank, Inc., to promise Sandoval a job for life, once he recovered. Sandoval was forced to retire with an outstanding record of 29 wins (17 knockouts) and 1 loss. In the image, Sandoval 's hand (center) is raised by the referee after posting a sixth-round TKO over David Bejines of Guadalajara, Jalisco, Mexico at the Olympic Auditorium on March 24, 1983. (Photograph by Carlos Baeza.)

Alberto "Tweety" Davila was a compact, crisp puncher who was managed by Howie Steindler (then later Bennie Georgino) and trained by Memo Soto. Davila had a pure boxing style and was a beautiful counterpuncher, leading Armando Muniz to say, "He's like Willie Pep. He can box." Davila fought from 1973 to 1988, ending with a record of 56 wins (26 knockouts) and 10 defeats. Davila won the vacant WBC bantamweight world championship in his fourth attempt at the title with a 12th-round knockout over "Kiko" Bejines of Guadalajara, Jalisco, Mexico, at the Olympic Auditorium on September 1, 1983. Davila's celebration was cut short when Bejines died three days later due to injuries suffered from the fight. Davila recalled to Dan Hanley, "Whatever the reasons, it turned tragic and what should have been my greatest night, turned into my worst." Davila is shown at the Main St. Gym before the "Kiko" Bejines fight. (Photograph by Carlos Baeza.)

Paul "Superfly" Gonzales, from East Los Angeles, set two important historical records before he ever stepped into the ring as a professional boxer. Gonzales became the first American to win an Olympic gold medal in the light flyweight division and the first Mexican American to capture a gold medal (in any sport) in the history of the Olympic Games. The Roosevelt High School graduate accomplished all of this in front of his hometown during the 1984 Summer Olympics in Los Angeles. Gonzales soon became an overnight hero and role model to every Latino kid in town. However, it was not an easy road for Gonzales, who grew up as one of eight children raised by a single mother, Anita, in the rough Aliso Village Housing Projects located in Boyle Heights. Gonzales was trained at the Hollenbeck Youth Center by Al Stankie, a Los Angeles cop and surrogate father to Paul. In the image, Gonzales (left) stands with promoter Don King at the Mike Tyson–Donovan Ruddock press conference in 1991 at the Mirage Hotel in Las Vegas. (Courtesy of Paul Gonzales.)

Above, Jaime Garza (left), touted as "The New West Coast Sensation," gets his hand raised by referee and former boxer Armando Muniz at the Olympic Auditorium during the early 1980s. Below, Garza (center), fighting out of Alhambra, proudly poses with his green WBC super bantamweight belt with manager Bennie Georgino (left) and trainer John Montes Sr. (right) at the Main St. Gym after winning the title in 1983. "El Rayo" ("Lightning") Garza took an undefeated record (40-0) into his second title defense at the Midtown Neighborhood Center in Kingston, New York, where he was brutally knocked out by Juan "Kid" Meza in a scintillating round one, losing his title on November 3, 1984. Garza was never the same, finishing his career with 48 wins (44 knockouts) and 6 losses while fighting from 1978 to 1995. (Above, courtesy of Armando Muniz; below, photograph by Carlos Baeza.)

Juan "Kid" Meza (fighting out of Los Angeles by way of Mexicali, Baja California, Mexico) was managed and trained by Jimmy Montoya. Meza became the first challenger in boxing history to get knocked down, get up, and become a new world champion, all in round one, by knocking out WBC super bantamweight titleholder Jaime Garza in their brief but fierce November 3, 1984, slugfest. Ted Sares of Boxing.com raved, "The fight took on the aura of a cockfight, with back and forth winging." Boxing writer Dan Hanley recounted, "(At) the pre-fight press luncheon . . . when Garza and Meza shook hands, Meza proceeded to tell Garza very explicitly what he intended to do to Garza's mother after the fight and quite obviously they had to be separated with Garza going after him. Garza then went outside and threw up. Of course the plan worked." Fighting from 1977 to 1997, the heavy-handed Meza posted a record of 45 wins (37 knockouts) and 9 losses. Photographer Carlos Baeza captured Meza in a solitary mood at the Olympic Gym in the early 1980s.

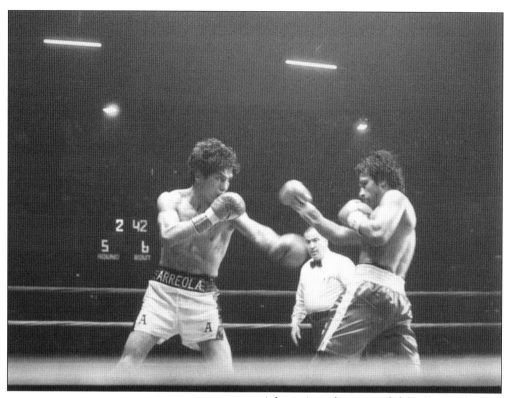

Adrian Arreola was a solid featherweight boxer from the gritty Aliso Village Housing Projects in Boyle Heights. Coming to the United States from Guadalajara, Jalisco, Mexico, when he was five years old, Arreola was managed and trained by Al Stankie while coached by Sonny Shapiro at the Hollenbeck Youth Center. Above, Arreola's greatest triumph in the ring was a dominating eight-round TKO over former WBC bantamweight champion Lupe Pintor (right) at the Olympic Auditorium on January 17, 1985, as referee Marty Denkin (center) keeps tabs on the action. Arreola said, "It was a big opportunity for me to fight a legend like Pintor and come out victorious." Arreola, shown at left relaxing before a fight at the Olympic Auditorium, fought from 1980 to 1992 and retired from boxing with a final record of 34 wins (17 knockouts) and 17 losses. (Both photographs by Carlos Baeza.)

BOXEO EN EL HISTORICO
OLYMPIC AUDITORIUM
NOV. 2
8 P.M.

VEA ESTA ENCARNIZADA BATALLA ENTRE DOS VALIENTES DEL RING:
UNO DE ALLA Y OTRO DE AQUI

10 ROUNDS — WELTERS

PIPINO CUEVAS -vs- HERMAN MONTES

TIENE
EL PODER PARA NOQUEAR A MONTES

ASEGURA
QUE LE GANARA A CUEVAS

10 ROUNDS — JR. WELTERS

RENE ARREDONDO -vs- "PANTERITA" CARVAJAL
MICHOACANO 3ro. JR. WELTER DEL MUNDO   COLOMBIANO INVICTO EN 20 PELEAS

10 ROUNDS — SUPERGALLOS

PAJARITO RICO -vs- VICTOR MORENO
APATZINGAN MICH.   CULIACAN SIN.

10 ROUNDS — JR. LIGERO

GUS OLMOS -vs- "SWEET" JAMES SOWELL
JR. LIGERO DE TIJUANA   VALIENTE MORENO DE LA AVE. CENTRAL

DE MEXICO
30 – 8 – 0 – 27 KO'S

DE LOS ANGELES
31 – 3 – 3 – 18 KO'S

PRECIOS DE BOLETOS RESERVADOS
$30.00 $25.00 y $20.00 AD. GEN. $15.00

DE VENTA TODOS LOS DIAS EN LAS TAQUILLAS DEL OLYMPIC
Y LIBRERIA MEXICO 311 So. BROADWAY L.A. C.A.
CASA PRIETO 1820 E. 1st. St. L.A. Tel. 261-8411

The evening of March 7, 1985 was filled with special circumstances when Herman "Kid" Montes met former WBA welterweight champion Pipino Cuevas at the Olympic Auditorium. Montes was facing his idol Cuevas (whose reign included 11 successful title defenses in four years), both wore red trunks, and as Montes left his corner he received some last-minute startling instructions from his father, "All right *mijo* (son), kill or be killed!" In the third round, both unleashed explosive left hooks simultaneously, but Montes's short left landed first and down went Cuevas for the count (administered by referee James Jen-Kin). The greatest moment in the career of "Kid" Montes was his knockout victory over the stone-faced assassin Cuevas of Mexico City. Below, Montes (right) celebrates with cornerman Danny "Little Red" Lopez (left) and his father/trainer John Montes Sr. (Both, courtesy of Herman Montes.)

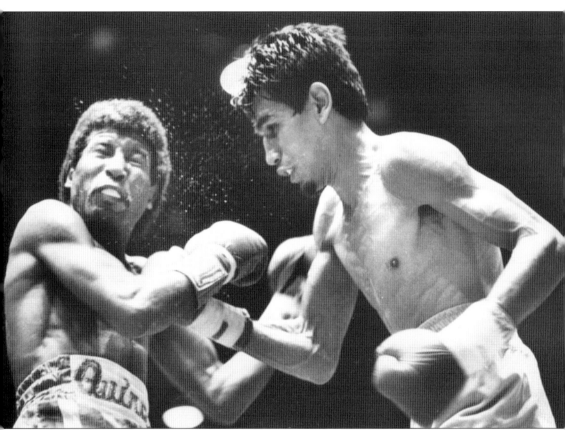

Joey Olivo, from East Los Angeles, became the first ever United States–born fighter to win the world light flyweight title. The long and winding road to the championship began in July 1984, when negotiations opened up for top contender Olivo to get a crack at the title in Miami, Florida. After several postponements, the purse bid moved the fight to a new location, Maracaibo, Venezuela, where Olivo put in five weeks of training. Near shoot-outs, gun-toting bodyguards, and constant tension surrounded Olivo as he was escorted by intimidating rifle-bearing soldiers. The next postponement moved the fight back to Florida, but it brought more bad news. The promoter revealed that Olivo's purse would only be $2,600. Before leaving Maracaibo, Olivo called his father, Joe Sr., for some familial advice and received his blessings to continue. After eight long months, Joey Olivo (right) took the WBA light flyweight title when he dethroned Francisco Quiroz (left) of the Dominican Republic with a 15-round unanimous decision at the Miami Beach Convention Center on March 29, 1985.

Joey Olivo (center) celebrates his world light flyweight championship at East Los Angeles nightclub the Pasta House in April 1985. Joining Olivo are 1984 Los Angeles Olympic Games gold medalist Paul Gonzales (left) and silver medalist (representing Mexico) Hector "El Torero" Lopez (right) of Glendale. Talk quickly surfaced of a million-dollar title fight between Olivo and Gonzales at East Los Angeles College Stadium, but, alas, it never happened. (Courtesy of Rudy Tellez.)

Don "War-a-Week" Chargin (center) was the matchmaker at the Olympic Auditorium from 1964 to 1984. Along with his wife, Lorraine, who began as building manager of the Olympic, Chargin promoted boxing shows all over the world for five decades. Bantamweight contender Richie Sandoval (left) of Pomona defeated George Garcia (right) of Westminster by a 10-round split decision on May 19, 1983, at the Los Angeles Sports Arena.

In Paul Gonzales's brief professional career from 1985 to 1991, he managed to win the WBA Continental Americas bantamweight title and set a record on February 2, 1986, for winning the NABF flyweight championship in only his third professional fight against Alonzo "Strongbow" Gonzalez at the Hollywood Palladium. In his fifth fight, Gonzales defended his NABF belt by unanimous decision over Orlando Canizales, of Laredo, Texas, on July 20, 1986, at Caesars Tahoe in Nevada. On June 10, 1990, Gonzales challenged Canizales again, but this time Canizales's IBF bantamweight title was at stake. Early in the bout, Gonzales suffered bad cuts over his left eye and lost by a second-round TKO at the County Coliseum in El Paso, Texas. Plagued by a brittle right hand, freak injuries, and managerial problems, Gonzales ended with a record of 16 wins (3 knockouts) and 4 losses. Gonzales (right) squares off with "The Greatest," Muhammad Ali, in 1987 at the Disneyland Hotel. In 2000, *Sports Illustrated* voted Gonzales onto its "Alltime Greatest U.S. Olympic Boxing Team" for the 106-pound light flyweight weight class. (Courtesy of Paul Gonzales.)

In 1984, after being away from boxing for three years, Frankie Duarte, 29, landed at Ten Goose Boxing in Van Nuys. Duarte was resurrected by manager Dan Goossen and trainer Joe Goossen, who guided him to a world title shot. Duarte (center) staggers WBA bantamweight champion Bernardo Pinango (left) of Venezuela in front of a celebrity-studded crowd at the Forum on February 3, 1987, as referee Hubert Earle (right) looks on. Even though Pinango was deducted three points for low blows and dropped by Duarte in the 12th, Duarte lost a bloody and controversial 15-round unanimous decision in another horrendous decision in boxing history. The key factor to the fight was the selection of judges, who were from Puerto Rico, Argentina, and Panama, as Duarte explained, "The WBA ruled that because I was not the mandatory No. 1 contender, we had no say in the judges. I figured I got robbed. After that fight I was never the same. I don't get the decision, but the next day I'm as big a hero as if I'd have won." (Courtesy of Frankie Duarte.)

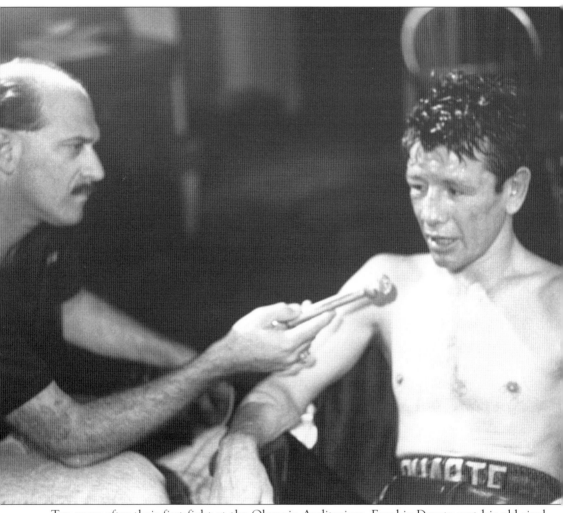

Ten years after their first fight at the Olympic Auditorium, Frankie Duarte met his old rival Alberto Davila once again. In the rematch, Davila dropped Duarte in the fourth round and was winning on all three judge's scorecards when referee Lou Filippo stopped the fight due to a bad cut on Davila's left eye. Duarte was awarded a 10-round TKO victory at the Forum on June 27, 1987, and recalled, "It was a tainted win. I was behind on points. I head-butted him, accidentally . . . of course. The referee didn't see the head-butt. I don't like winning fights that way. I don't want Davila to look at me and say 'there's that guy who thinks he beat me.' As it stands, Davila got burned. It's hard for me to say that. I want him to know I don't claim I beat him. For some reason God has used Davila to humble me. I take that fight as a loss. I want Davila to know that." Here, Duarte is interviewed by sportscaster Rick Marotta in 1987. (Courtesy of Frankie Duarte.)

Seven

THE 1990S
THERE'S A NEW GOLDEN BOY IN TOWN

Never saw him [Oscar De La Hoya] fight before, not on TV, never. For a long time, I didn't want to see him, but then before this fight, I asked somebody how much he was gonna make. They said $9 million. I said they can call him anything they want.

—Art Aragon, the original "Golden Boy," as told to Bill Dwyre, *Los Angeles Times*

Like the Beatles rock 'n' roll phenomenon, an Oscar De La Hoya only comes around once in a lifetime. Easily the most famous and successful of all Mexican American boxers in Los Angeles, this 10-time world champion (in six different weight classes) transcended boxing to stretch out into the realm of popular culture. De La Hoya broke down boundaries of the boxing world, becoming a Grammy-nominated recording artist, book author, and television host. He attracted more women than men to his bout in El Paso, Texas, began a clothing line, received praise for his community charity efforts, and eventually developed into a world-class boxing promoter.

Michael Leahy writes in his article, "The Not-So-Sweet Science of Selling Oscar De La Hoya" for *Los Angeles Times Magazine*: "He had been coveted by shrewd boxing men who saw millions to be made on a kid whose teen-idol looks, fast hands and mule-kicking left hook would merely complement his most marketable feature: the ineffable mix of his American citizenship and Mexican ancestry."

Coming from a boxing family to win Olympic Gold in 1992, he was quickly tagged by the press as "The Golden Boy." Many tears were shed when De La Hoya fulfilled his personal promise to win a gold medal for his mother, Cecilia, who had passed away in 1990.

As a professional, "The Pride of East L.A." carried the decade on his shoulders, beating a who's who of world champions in the 1990s. "The Golden Boy" was undefeated (31-0) until he tasted his first loss against Felix "Tito" Trinidad of Puerto Rico on September 18, 1999, in Las Vegas, Nevada. He was ahead on points going into the late rounds, and many believe De La Hoya received some bad corner advice that resulted in an unnecessary loss.

Oscar De La Hoya, East Los Angeles' native son, won the gold medal in the lightweight division at the 1992 Olympic Games in Barcelona, Spain, and celebrated his victory by carrying two flags around the ring. He told *Los Angeles Magazine*, "The American flag was for my country, the Mexican flag for my heritage." Two stories exist on the naming of "The Golden Boy": John Beyrooty (former sportswriter for the *Los Angeles Herald Examiner* newspaper) put it in print during a public relations stint at the Forum, and De La Hoya's uncle Vicente claims to have started it at the Barcelona Olympic Games. A 19-year-old De La Hoya made his professional debut only three months after winning the gold medal when he knocked out Lamar Williams of Eric, Pennsylvania, in the first round at the Great Western Forum on November 23, 1992. Cutman Joe Chavez remembers a young De La Hoya: "You could tell he was special. He had that eye of the tiger."

The year 1994 was memorable for brothers Rafael Ruelas (left) and Gabriel Ruelas (right) as trainer Joe Goossen (center) and manager Dan Goossen guided them both to world championships. Born in Yerbabuena, Jalisco, Mexico, but growing up in Sylmar, California, the brothers sold candy door-to-door as young children to help make ends meet. When Gabriel was 12 and Rafael 11, they stumbled into the Ten Goose Boxing Gym in North Hollywood, where Alonzo "Strongbow" Gonzalez (the No. 1 flyweight contender) persuaded Joe Goosen to take Gabriel in because "he saw something in his eyes." Rafael won the IBF lightweight championship on February 19, 1994, with a 12-round unanimous decision over titleholder "Fearless" Freddie Pendleton at the Forum and retired with a record of 53 wins (42 knockouts) and 4 losses while fighting from 1989 to 1999. Gabriel defeated champion Jesse James Leija, of San Antonio, Texas, by a 12-round unanimous decision to win the WBC super featherweight championship on September 17, 1994, at the MGM Grand in Las Vegas and fought from 1988 to 2003, ending with a record of 49 wins (24 knockouts) and 7 losses.

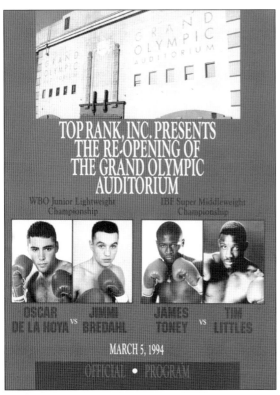

Oscar De La Hoya, a Garfield High School graduate, told David A. Avila of Maxboxing.com, "That's where I'm from. I love East L.A." De La Hoya is a third-generation boxer who followed in the footsteps of his grandfather Vicente (a featherweight from Durango, Mexico, in the 1940s) and his father, Joel Sr. (a lightweight in the mid-1960s). Below, before a hometown crowd at the Olympic Auditorium on March 5, 1994, "The Golden Boy" (left) scored a 10-round TKO over defending WBO junior lightweight champion Jimmi Bredahl (right) of Denmark for his first world title in only his 12th professional fight. *Los Angeles Times* sports columnist Jim Murray wrote, "Now, there's a Golden Boy in the 90s. Oscar De La Hoya is a gladiator of the old school. He takes his nickname and his profession seriously. He wants to be the best there is in his cruel trade." (Left, courtesy of Top Rank, Inc.; below, photograph by Brent Cook.)

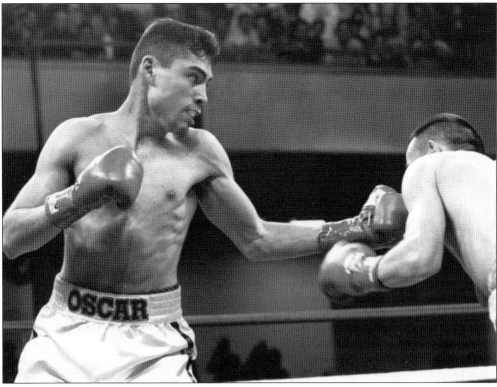

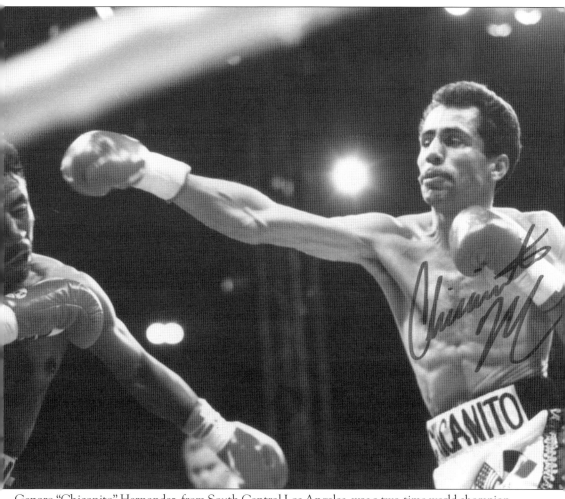

Genaro "Chicanito" Hernandez, from South Central Los Angeles, was a two-time world champion comanaged by Nori Takatani and father Rodolfo Hernandez while trained by older brother and former boxer Rudy "Chicano" Hernandez. A workingman's champion, Genaro won the vacant WBA super featherweight title by a ninth-round TKO over Daniel Londas of France at Complex Sport le COMEP, Epernay, Marne, France, on November 22, 1991. "Chicanito" proceeded to defend his belt eight times until 1994, when he vacated his crown to take on WBO lightweight champion Oscar De La Hoya at Caesars Palace on September 9, 1995, but lost to "The Golden Boy" by a sixth-round TKO. A couple of years later, Hernandez captured the WBC version of the super featherweight title with a memorable victory over defending champion Azumah Nelson "The Professor" of Accra, Ghana, on March 22, 1997, at the Memorial Coliseum in Corpus Christi, Texas. "Chicanito" was ahead on all three scorecards when Nelson landed a shot to Hernandez's throat after the bell had sounded to end the seventh round. Hernandez went down, hurt, and was promised the title by WBC czar Jose Sulaiman, as Nelson would be disqualified for his foul. "Chicanito" refused the offer, choosing to fight on, and won the championship in the ring "like real champions do" by a 12-round split decision—which he followed with three successful title defenses. In a 14-year career that lasted from 1984 to 1998, "Chicanito" retired with a record of 38 wins (17 knockouts), 2 losses (from Oscar De La Hoya and Floyd Mayweather Jr.), and 1 draw. In the image, "Chicanito" throws a long right at Jimmy Garcia (left) of Colombia while defending his WBA title with a 12-round unanimous decision victory at Plaza Mexico, Mexico City, on November 12, 1994.

In a battle for Los Angeles' lightweight supremacy, Oscar De La Hoya, "The Golden Boy" of East Los Angeles and WBO lightweight champion, took on Rafael Ruelas of Sylmar, California, the IBF lightweight champion, in a Cinco de Mayo weekend duel at Caesars Palace in Las Vegas. De La Hoya carried in a 17-0 record with 15 knockouts, while Ruelas was 43-1 with 34 knockouts at the time of their May 6, 1995, title unification bout. De La Hoya won territorial bragging rights and picked up another belt in an electrifying second-round knockout of Ruelas. Raul Jaimes, vice president of Golden Boy Promotions, recalled to David A. Avila of Maxboxing.com, "People forget that he was an underdog against Rafael Ruelas. When he knocked out Ruelas so easy, the people didn't know what to do. Those same people that booed him suddenly realized he could really fight. That was the big turning point." (Courtesy of Top Rank, Inc.)

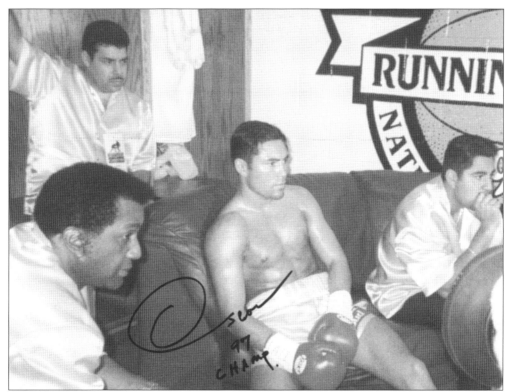

On Mexican Independence Day weekend, "The Golden Boy" Oscar De La Hoya defended his WBC welterweight title against flamboyant former world champion Hector "Macho" Camacho of Bayamon, Puerto Rico, at Thomas & Mack Center in Las Vegas. De La Hoya had Camacho down in the ninth round en route to a 12-round unanimous decision on September 13, 1997. Above, in the dressing room, De La Hoya (center) gets into the zone for the Camacho fight with trainer Robert Alcazar (back left), trainer Emanuel Steward (front left), and brother/cornerman Joel De La Hoya (front right). Below, De La Hoya (left) is in the dressing room with Raul Jaimes (center), vice president of Golden Boy Promotions, and Jack Lazzarotto (right), inspector from the Nevada State Athletic Commission. After fighting from 1992 to 2008, De La Hoya retired with a final record of 39 wins (30 knockouts) and 6 losses.

APPENDIX

These tables show the weight class divisions, sanctioning bodies, and Mexican American boxers from the Los Angeles area who have been inducted into the hall of fame.

WEIGHT CLASS DIVISIONS

Heavyweights	over 200 pounds
Cruiserweights	not over 200 pounds
Light Heavyweights	not over 175 pounds
Super Middleweights	not over 168 pounds
Middleweights	not over 160 pounds
Junior Middleweights	not over 154 pounds (Super Welterweights by the WBC and WBA)
Welterweights	not over 147 pounds
Junior Welterweights	not over 140 pounds (Super Lightweights by the WBC and WBA)
Lightweights	not over 135 pounds
Junior Lightweights	not over 130 pounds (Super Featherweights by the WBC and WBA)
Featherweights	not over 126 pounds
Junior Featherweights	not over 122 pounds (Super Bantamweights by the WBC and WBA)
Bantamweights	not over 118 pounds
Junior Bantamweights	not over 115 pounds (Super Flyweights by the WBC and WBA)
Flyweights	not over 112 pounds
Junior Flyweights	not over 108 pounds (Light Flyweights by the WBC and WBA)
Strawweights (WBC)	not over 105 pounds (Minimumweights by the WBA, Mini Flyweights by the IBF and WBO)

SANCTIONING BODIES

NYSAC: New York State Athletic Commission (established in 1920)
NBA: National Boxing Association (established in 1921, changed to WBA in 1962)
WBA: World Boxing Association (established in 1962)
WBC: World Boxing Council (established in 1963)
IBF: International Boxing Federation (established in 1984)
WBO: World Boxing Organization (established in 1988)
NABF: North American Boxing Federation (established in 1969, affiliated with the WBC)
USBA: United States Boxing Association (established in 1976, affiliated with the IBF)

INDUCTEES TO INTERNATIONAL BOXING HALL OF FAME, CANASTOTA, NEW YORK

1996:   Manuel Ortiz (July 2, 1916–May 31, 1970)
2004:   Alberto "Baby" Arizmendi (March 17, 1914–December 31, 1963)
        Carlos Palomino (August 10, 1949–)
2005:   Bobby Chacon (November 28, 1951–)
2010:   Danny "Little Red" Lopez (July 6, 1952–)
2014:   Oscar De La Hoya (February 4, 1973–)